I0415724

Weather and Climate Inventory National Park Service Gulf Coast Network

Natural Resource Technical Report NPS/GULN/NRTR—2007/011
WRCC Report 2007-07

Christopher A. Davey, Kelly T. Redmond, and David B. Simeral
Western Regional Climate Center
Desert Research Institute
2215 Raggio Parkway
Reno, Nevada 89512-1095

April 2007

U.S. Department of the Interior
National Park Service
Natural Resource Program Center
Fort Collins, Colorado

The Natural Resource Publication series addresses natural resource topics that are of interest and applicability to a broad readership in the National Park Service and to others in the management of natural resources, including the scientific community, the public, and the National Park Service conservation and environmental constituencies. Manuscripts are peer-reviewed to ensure that the information is scientifically credible, technically accurate, appropriately written for the intended audience, and designed and published in a professional manner.

The Natural Resources Technical Reports series is used to disseminate the peer-reviewed results of scientific studies in the physical, biological, and social sciences for both the advancement of science and the achievement of the National Park Service mission. The reports provide contributors with a forum for displaying comprehensive data that are often deleted from journals because of page limitations. Current examples of such reports include the results of research that address natural resource management issues; natural resource inventory and monitoring activities; resource assessment reports; scientific literature reviews; and peer-reviewed proceedings of technical workshops, conferences, or symposia.

Views and conclusions in this report are those of the authors and do not necessarily reflect policies of the National Park Service. Mention of trade names or commercial products does not constitute endorsement or recommendation for use by the National Park Service.

Printed copies of reports in these series may be produced in a limited quantity and they are only available as long as the supply lasts. This report is also available from the Natural Resource Publications Management website (http://www.nature.nps.gov/publications/NRPM) on the Internet or by sending a request to the address on the back cover.

Please cite this publication as follows:

Davey, C. A., K. T. Redmond, and D. B. Simeral. 2007. Weather and Climate Inventory, National Park Service, Gulf Coast Network. Natural Resource Technical Report NPS/GULN/NRTR—2007/011. National Park Service, Fort Collins, Colorado.

NPS/GULN/NRTR—2007/011, April 2007

Contents

Contents (continued)

Figures

Tables

Appendixes

Acronyms

AASC	American Association of State Climatologists
ACIS	Applied Climate Information System
ASOS	Automated Surface Observing System
AWOS	Automated Weather Observing System
BITH	Big Thicket National Preserve
BLM	Bureau of Land Management
CASTNet	Clean Air Status and Trends Network
COOP	Cooperative Observer Program
CRN	NOAA Climate Reference Network
CWOP	Citizen Weather Observer Program
DFIR	Double-Fence Intercomparison Reference
DST	daylight savings time
ENSO	El Niño Southern Oscillation
EPA	Environmental Protection Agency
FAA	Federal Aviation Administration
FIPS	Federal Information Processing Standards
GMT	Greenwich Mean Time
GOES	Geostationary Operational Environmental Satellite
GPMP	Gaseous Pollutant Monitoring Program
GPS	Global Positioning System
GPS-MET	NOAA ground-based GPS meteorology
GUIS	Gulf Islands National Seashore
GULN	Gulf Coast Inventory and Monitoring Network
I&M	NPS Inventory and Monitoring Program
JELA	Jean Lafitte National Historical Park and Preserve
LEO	Low Earth Orbit
LST	local standard time
MDN	Mercury Deposition Network
MEXICO	Mexico weather/climate stations
NADP	National Atmospheric Deposition Program
NASA	National Aeronautics and Space Administration
NATR	Natchez Trace Parkway
NCDC	National Climatic Data Center
NetCDF	Network Common Data Form
NOAA	National Oceanic and Atmospheric Administration
NPS	National Park Service
NRCS	Natural Resources Conservation Service
NWS	National Weather Service
PAAL	Palo Alto Battlefield National Historic Site
PAIS	Padre Island National Seashore
POMS	Portable Ozone Monitoring System
PRISM	Parameter Regression on Independent Slopes Model
RAWS	Remote Automated Weather Station network
RCC	regional climate center

SAAN	San Antonio Missions National Historical Park
SAO	Surface Airways Observation network
SCAN	Soil Climate Analysis Network
SNOTEL	Snowfall Telemetry network
SOD	Summary Of the Day
Surfrad	Surface Radiation Budget network
USDA	U.S. Department of Agriculture
USGS	U.S. Geological Survey
UTC	Coordinated Universal Time
VICK	Vicksburg National Military Park
WBAN	Weather Bureau Army Navy
WMO	World Meteorological Organization
WRCC	Western Regional Climate Center
WX4U	Weather For You network

Executive Summary

Climate is a dominant factor driving the physical and ecologic processes affecting the Gulf Coast Inventory and Monitoring Network (GULN), which contains a broad range of upland, freshwater, and coastal ecosystems, including the most extensive wetland areas in the U.S. Compared to other networks, the GULN is uniquely vulnerable to potential sea level rises due to future climate changes, as these rises would inundate substantial tracts of valuable coastal wetlands, particularly in Louisiana. Occasional drought periods can have significant negative consequences on GULN ecosystems, since many of these systems are very dependent on water availability. Future climate changes may lead to more frequent drought conditions across much of the GULN. Tropical storms and hurricanes regularly make landfall along the Gulf Coast during the summer and fall months, playing a significant role in shaping the structure and characteristics of GULN ecosystems, particularly coastal systems. Human influences have introduced disturbances and land-use heterogeneities that have introduced local- and regional-scale climate changes and adversely affect the ability of the plant and animal communities in the GULN to adapt to future climate changes and compete successfully with newly-established non-native species. Because of its influence on the ecology of GULN park units and the surrounding areas, climate was identified as a high-priority vital sign for GULN and is one of the 12 basic inventories to be completed for all National Park Service (NPS) Inventory and Monitoring Program (I&M) networks.

This project was initiated to inventory past and present climate monitoring efforts. In this report, we provide the following information:

- Overview of broad-scale climatic factors and zones important to GULN park units.
- Inventory of weather and climate station locations in and near GULN park units relevant to the NPS I&M Program.
- Results of an inventory of metadata on each weather station, including affiliations for weather-monitoring networks, types of measurements recorded at these stations, and information about the actual measurements (length of record, etc.).
- Initial evaluation of the adequacy of coverage for existing weather stations and recommendations for improvements in monitoring weather and climate.

The GULN climate results from the interplay of regional factors, such as its latitude and the influence of nearby water bodies, and global factors that include the El Niño Southern Oscillation (ENSO). The GULN region experiences mild to warm conditions year-round. Mean annual precipitation is greatest along and just inland of the east-central Gulf Coast, and it ranges from under 800 mm for the park units in southern Texas to over 1600 mm for park units along coastal Louisiana and Mississippi. The seasonal timing of precipitation varies greatly throughout the GULN. The western Gulf Coast is wettest in late summer and early fall, the central and eastern Gulf Coast is wettest from late spring through summer, and inland locations tend to be wettest in winter and spring. Mean annual temperatures in the GULN are warmest for park units closest to the Gulf of Mexico. In southern Texas, these temperatures can average above 22°C. The coolest conditions are generally found along northern portions of the Natchez Trace Parkway (NATR), where mean annual temperatures are less than 12°C. January temperatures have approached -20°C along northern portions of NATR during severe cold snaps, while July maximum temperatures around San Antonio Missions National Historical Park (SAAN) have reached as high as 45°C.

Through a search of national databases and inquiries to NPS staff, we have identified 17 weather and climate stations within GULN park units. Gulf Islands National Seashore (GUIS) has the most stations within park unit boundaries (six).

Two park units within the GULN have areas of little or no weather/climate station coverage that could be addressed. Padre Island National Seashore (PAIS) currently has no coverage within the main portion of Padre Island, nor are there any available stations at inland locations to the west of the park unit. Almost all of the available weather/climate stations are located within 30 km of either the north tip of PAIS (Corpus Christi area) or at the south tip of PAIS (Port Mansfield and nearby communities). The six stations identified for GUIS are all in the eastern portions of GULN, along the Florida Panhandle; the western islands of GUIS have no stations on them. There are still plenty of weather and climate stations along the Mississippi coast that can provide data for the western island units of GUIS; however, this does not help in monitoring local conditions at the island units themselves.

Two parks units in the GULN, PAAL and SAAN, have no weather/climate stations within their park boundaries. These park units must rely heavily on outside sources of weather and climate data. Fortunately, both long-term and near-real-time stations are available for PAAL and SAAN.

A few of the parks units of the GULN have anywhere from one to at most a few weather and/or climate stations within the park unit. These park units include BITH, JELA, and VICK. Despite having these valuable stations, the park units in this category must still rely heavily on outside sources of weather and climate data. For all three of these park units, we have deemed the coverage outside the park units of both near-real-time weather stations and long-term climate stations to be satisfactory for addressing GULN weather- and climate-monitoring objectives. The expansion of weather-monitoring efforts at BITH could be considered, as it is comprised of several units, only one of which currently has any ongoing weather monitoring (Turkey Creek unit: one RAWS station). Since the RAWS network already has a presence in the BITH region, NPS may benefit by considering working with local officials to install additional RAWS stations at other BITH units.

Acknowledgements

This work was supported and completed under Task Agreement H8R07010001, with the Great Basin Cooperative Ecosystem Studies Unit. We would like to acknowledge very helpful assistance from various National Park Service personnel associated with the Gulf Coast Inventory and Monitoring Network. Particular thanks are extended to Martha Segura and Whitney Granger. We also thank John Gross, Margaret Beer, Grant Kelly, Greg McCurdy, and Heather Angeloff for all their help. Seth Gutman with the National Oceanic and Atmospheric Administration Earth Systems Research Laboratory provided valuable input on the GPS-MET station network. Portions of the work were supported by the NOAA Western Regional Climate Center.

1.0. Introduction

Weather and climate are key drivers in ecosystem structure and function. Global- and regional-scale climate variations will have a tremendous impact on natural systems (Chapin et al. 1996; Schlesinger 1997; Jacobson et al. 2000; Bonan 2002). Long-term patterns in temperature and precipitation provide first-order constraints on potential ecosystem structure and function. Secondary constraints are realized from the intensity and duration of individual weather events and, additionally, from seasonality and inter-annual climate variability. These constraints influence the fundamental properties of ecologic systems, such as soil–water relationships, plant–soil processes, and nutrient cycling, as well as disturbance rates and intensity. These properties, in turn, influence the life-history strategies supported by a climatic regime (Neilson 1987; Segura et al. 2005).

Given the importance of climate, it is one of 12 basic inventories to be completed by the National Park Service (NPS) Inventory and Monitoring Program (I&M) network (I&M 2006). As primary environmental drivers for the other vital signs, weather and climate patterns present various practical and management consequences and implications for the NPS (Oakley et al. 2003). Most park units observe weather and climate elements as part of their overall mission. The lands under NPS stewardship provide many excellent locations for monitoring climatic conditions.

It is essential that park units within the Gulf Coast Inventory and Monitoring Network (GULN) have an effective climate-monitoring system in place to track climate changes and to aid in management decisions relating to these changes. The purpose of this report is to determine the current status of weather and climate monitoring within the GULN (Table 1.1; Figure 1.1). In this report, we provide the following informational elements:

- Overview of broad-scale climatic factors and zones important to GULN park units.
- Inventory of locations for all weather stations in and near GULN park units that are relevant to the NPS I&M networks.
- Results of metadata inventory for each station, including weather-monitoring network affiliations, types of recorded measurements, and information about actual measurements (length of record, etc.).
- Initial evaluation of the adequacy of coverage for existing weather stations and recommendations for improvements in monitoring weather and climate.

The primary objectives for climate- and weather-monitoring in the GULN are as follows (Segura et al. 2005):

A. Understand the natural range and variation in weather patterns and climate trends across the GULN parks.
B. Establish baseline conditions for all other vital signs.

1.1. Network Terminology
Before proceeding, it is important to stress that this report discusses the idea of "networks" in two different ways. Modifiers are used to distinguish between NPS I&M networks and weather/climate station networks. See Appendix A for a full definition of these terms.

1

1.1.1. Weather/Climate Station Networks

Most weather and climate measurements are made not from isolated stations but from stations that are part of a network operated in support of a particular mission. The limiting case is a network of one station, where measurements are made by an interested observer or group. Larger networks usually have additional inventory data and station-tracking procedures. Some national weather/climate networks are associated with the National Oceanic and Atmospheric Administration (NOAA), including the National Weather Service (NWS) Cooperative Observer Program (COOP). Other national networks include the interagency Remote Automated Weather Station network (RAWS) and the U.S. Department of Agriculture/Natural Resources Conservation Service (USDA/NRCS) Soil Climate Analysis Network (SCAN). Usually a single agency, but sometimes a consortium of interested parties, will jointly support a particular weather/climate network.

Table 1.1. Park units in the Gulf Coast Network.

Acronym	Name
BITH	Big Thicket National Preserve
GUIS	Gulf Islands National Seashore
JELA	Jean Lafitte National Historical Park and Preserve
NATR	Natchez Trace Parkway
PAAL	Palo Alto Battlefield National Historic Site
PAIS	Padre Island National Seashore
SAAN	San Antonio Missions National Historical Park
VICK	Vicksburg National Military Park

1.1.2. NPS I&M Networks

Within the NPS, the system for monitoring various attributes in the participating park units (about 270–280 in total) is divided into 32 NPS I&M networks. These networks are collections of park units grouped together around a common theme, typically geographical.

1.2. Weather versus Climate Definitions

It is also important to distinguish whether the primary use of a given station is for weather purposes or for climate purposes. Weather station networks are intended for near-real-time usage, where the precise circumstances of a set of measurements are typically less important. In these cases, changes in exposure or other attributes over time are not as critical. Climate networks, however, are intended for long-term tracking of atmospheric conditions. Siting and exposure are critical factors for climate networks, and it is vitally important that the observational circumstances remain essentially unchanged over the duration of the station record.

Some climate networks can be considered hybrids of weather/climate networks. These hybrid climate networks can supply information on a short-term "weather" time scale and a longer-term "climate" time scale.

In this report, "weather" generally refers to current (or near-real-time) atmospheric conditions, while "climate" is defined as the complete ensemble of statistical descriptors for temporal and

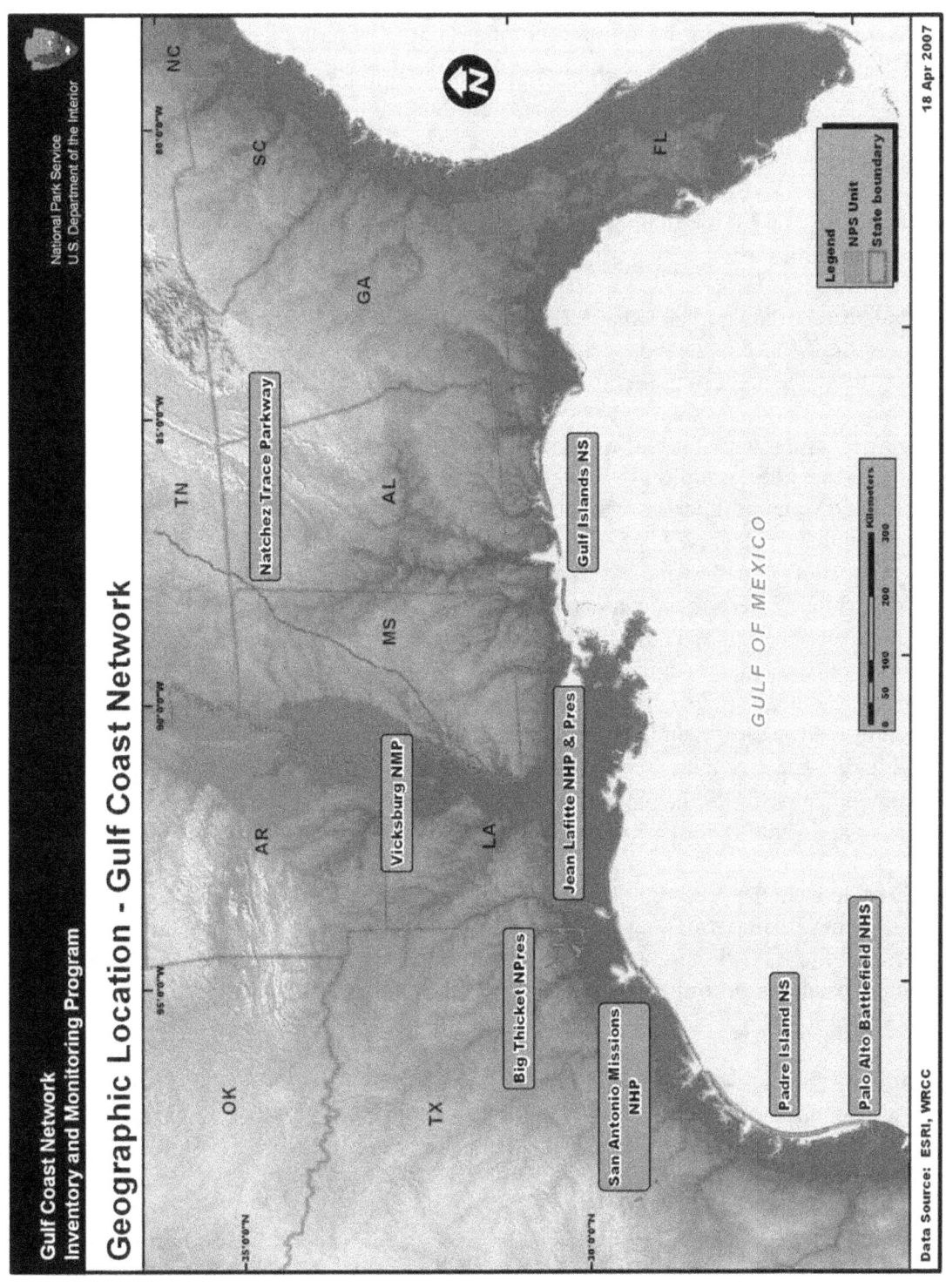

Figure 1.1. Map of the Gulf Coast Network.

spatial properties of atmospheric behavior (see Appendix A). Climate and weather phenomena shade gradually into each other and are ultimately inseparable.

1.3. Purpose of Measurements

Climate inventory and monitoring climate activities should be based on a set of guiding fundamental principles. Any evaluation of weather/climate monitoring programs begins with asking the following question:

- What is the purpose of weather and climate measurements?

Evaluation of past, present, or planned weather/climate monitoring activities must be based on the answer to this question.

Weather and climate data and information constitute a prominent and widely requested component of the NPS I&M networks (I&M 2006). Within the context of the NPS, the following services constitute the main purposes for recording weather and climate observations:

- Provide measurements for real-time operational needs and early warnings of potential hazards (landslides, mudflows, washouts, fallen trees, plowing activities, fire conditions, aircraft and watercraft conditions, road conditions, rescue conditions, fog, restoration and remediation activities, etc.).
- Provide visitor education and aid interpretation of expected and actual conditions for visitors while they are in the park and for deciding if and when to visit the park.
- Establish engineering and design criteria for structures, roads, culverts, etc., for human comfort, safety, and economic needs.
- Consistently monitor climate over the long-term to detect changes in environmental drivers affecting ecosystems, including both gradual and sudden events.
- Provide retrospective data to understand *a posteriori* changes in flora and fauna.
- Document for posterity the physical conditions in and near the park units, including mean, extreme, and variable measurements (in time and space) for all applications.

The last three items in the preceding list are pertinent primarily to the NPS I&M networks; however, all items are important to NPS operations and management. Most of the needs in this list overlap heavily. It is often impractical to operate separate climate measuring systems that also cannot be used to meet ordinary weather needs, where there is greater emphasis on timeliness and reliability.

1.4. Design of Climate-Monitoring Programs

Determining the purposes for collecting measurements in a given weather/climate monitoring program will guide the process of identifying weather/climate stations suitable for the monitoring program. The context for making these decisions is provided in Chapter 2 where background on the GULN climate is presented. However, this process is only one step in evaluating and designing a climate-monitoring program. This process includes the following additional steps:

- Define park and network-specific monitoring needs and objectives.
- Identify locations and data repositories of existing and historic stations.

4

- Acquire existing data when necessary or practical.
- Evaluate the quality of existing data.
- Evaluate the adequacy of coverage of existing stations.
- Develop a protocol for monitoring the weather and climate, including the following:
    o Standardized summaries and reports of weather/climate data.
    o Data management (quality assurance and quality control, archiving, data access, etc.).
- Develop and implement a plan for installing or modifying stations, as necessary.

Throughout the design process, there are various factors that require consideration in evaluating weather and climate measurements. Many of these factors have been summarized by Dr. Tom Karl, director of the NOAA National Climatic Data Center (NCDC), and widely distributed as the "Ten Principles for Climate Monitoring" (Karl et al. 1996; NRC 2001). These principals are presented in Appendix B, and the guidelines are embodied in many of the comments made throughout this report. The most critical factors are presented here. In addition, an overview of requirements necessary to operate a climate network is provided in Appendix C, with further discussion in Appendix D.

1.4.1. Need for Consistency
A principal goal in climate monitoring is to detect and characterize slow and sudden changes in climate through time. This is of less concern for day-to-day weather changes, but it is of paramount importance for climate variability and change. There are many ways whereby changes in techniques for making measurements, changes in instruments or their exposures, or seemingly innocuous changes in site characteristics can lead to apparent changes in climate. Safeguards must be in place to avoid these false sources of temporal "climate" variability if we are to draw correct inferences about climate behavior over time from archived measurements.

For climate monitoring, consistency through time is vital, counting at least as important as absolute accuracy. Sensors record only what is occurring at the sensor—this is all they can detect. It is the responsibility of station or station network managers to ensure that observations are representative of the spatial and temporal climate scales that we wish to record.

1.4.2. Metadata
Changes in instruments, site characteristics, and observing methodologies can lead to apparent changes in climate through time. It is therefore vital to document all factors that can bear on the interpretation of climate measurements and to update the information repeatedly through time. This information ("metadata," data about data) has its own history and set of quality-control issues that parallel those of the actual data. There is no single standard for the content of climate metadata, but a simple rule suffices:

- Observers should record all information that could be needed in the future to interpret observations correctly without benefit of the observers' personal recollections.

Such documentation includes notes, drawings, site forms, and photos, which can be of inestimable value if taken in the correct manner. That stated, it is not always clear to the metadata provider *what is important* for posterity and *what will be important* in the future. It is almost impossible to "over document" a station. Station documentation is greatly underappreciated and is seldom thorough enough (especially for climate purposes). Insufficient attention to this issue often lowers the present and especially future value of otherwise useful data.

The convention followed throughout climatology is to refer to metadata as information about the measurement process, station circumstances, and data. The term "data" is reserved solely for the actual weather and climate records obtained from sensors.

1.4.3. Maintenance

Inattention to maintenance is the greatest source of failure in weather/climate stations and networks. Problems begin to occur soon after sites are deployed. A regular visit schedule must be implemented, where sites, settings (e.g., vegetation), sensors, communications, and data flow are checked routinely (once or twice a year at a minimum) and updated as necessary. Parts must be changed out for periodic recalibration or replacement. With adequate maintenance, the entire instrument suite should be replaced or completely refurbished about once every five to seven years.

Simple preventative maintenance is effective but requires much planning and skilled technical staff. Changes in technology and products require retraining and continual re-education. Travel, logistics, scheduling, and seasonal access restrictions consume major amounts of time and budget but are absolutely necessary. Without such attention, data gradually become less credible and then often are misused or not used at all.

1.4.4. Automated versus Manual Stations

Historic stations often have depended on manual observations and many continue to operate in this mode. Manual observations frequently produce excellent data sets. Sensors and data are simple and intuitive, well tested, and relatively cheap. Manual stations have much to offer in certain circumstances and can be a source of both primary and backup data. However, methodical consistency for manual measurements is a constant challenge, especially with a mobile work force. Operating manual stations takes time and needs to be done on a regular schedule, though sometimes the routine is welcome.

Nearly all newer stations are automated. Automated stations provide better time resolution, increased (though imperfect) reliability, greater capacity for data storage, and improved accessibility to large amounts of data. The purchase cost for automated stations is higher than for manual stations. A common expectation and serious misconception is that an automated station can be deployed and left to operate on its own. In reality, automation does not eliminate the need for people but rather changes the type of person that is needed. Skilled technical personnel are needed and must be readily available, especially if live communications exist and data gaps are not wanted. Site visits are needed at least annually and spare parts must be maintained. Typical annual costs for sensors and maintenance at the major national networks are $1500–2500 per station per year but these costs still can vary greatly depending on the kind of automated site.

1.4.5. Communications

With manual stations, the observer is responsible for recording and transmitting station data. Data from automated stations, however, can be transmitted quickly for access by research and operations personnel, which is a highly preferable situation. A comparison of communication systems for automated and manual stations shows that automated stations generally require additional equipment, more power, higher transmission costs, attention to sources of disruption or garbling, and backup procedures (e.g. manual downloads from data loggers).

Automated stations are capable of functioning normally without communication and retaining many months of data. At such sites, however, alerts about station problems are not possible, large gaps can accrue when accessible stations quit, and the constituencies needed to support such stations are smaller and less vocal. Two-way communications permit full recovery from disruptions, ability to reprogram data loggers remotely, and better opportunities for diagnostics and troubleshooting. In virtually all cases, two-way communications are much preferred to all other communication methods. However, two-way communications require considerations of cost, signal access, transmission rates, interference, and methods for keeping sensor and communication power loops separate. Two-way communications are frequently impossible (no service) or impractical, expensive, or power consumptive. Two-way methods (cellular, land line, radio, Internet) require smaller up-front costs as compared to other methods of communication and have variable recurrent costs, starting at zero. Satellite links work everywhere (except when blocked by trees or cliffs) and are quite reliable but are one-way and relatively slow, allow no re-transmissions, and require high up-front costs ($3000–4000) but no recurrent costs. Communications technology is changing constantly and requires vigilant attention by maintenance personnel.

1.4.6. Quality Assurance and Quality Control

Quality control and quality assurance are issues at every step through the entire sequence of sensing, communication, storage, retrieval, and display of environmental data. Quality assurance is an umbrella concept that covers all data collection and processing (start-to-finish) and ensures that credible information is available to the end user. Quality control has a more limited scope and is defined by the International Standards Organization as "the operational techniques and activities that are used to satisfy quality requirements." The central problem can be better appreciated if we approach quality control in the following way.

- Quality control is the evaluation, assessment, and rehabilitation of imperfect data by utilizing other imperfect data.

The quality of the data only decreases with time once the observation is made. The best and most effective quality control, therefore, consists in making high-quality measurements from the start and then successfully transmitting the measurements to an ingest process and storage site. Once the data are received from a monitoring station, a series of checks with increasing complexity can be applied, ranging from single-element checks (self-consistency) to multiple-element checks (inter-sensor consistency) to multiple-station/single-element checks (inter-station consistency). Suitable ancillary data (battery voltages, data ranges for all measurements, etc.) can prove extremely useful in diagnosing problems.

There is rarely a single technique in quality control procedures that will work satisfactorily for all situations. Quality-control procedures must be tailored to individual station circumstances, data access and storage methods, and climate regimes.

The fundamental issue in quality control centers on the tradeoff between falsely rejecting good data (Type I error) and falsely accepting bad data (Type II error). We cannot reduce the incidence of one type of error without increasing the incidence of the other type. In weather and climate data assessments, since good data are absolutely crucial for interpreting climate records properly, Type I errors are deemed far less desirable than Type II errors.

Not all observations are equal in importance. Quality-control procedures are likely to have the greatest difficulty evaluating the most extreme observations, where independent information usually must be sought and incorporated. Quality-control procedures involving more than one station usually involve a great deal of infrastructure with its own (imperfect) error-detection methods, which must be in place before a single value can be evaluated.

1.4.7. Standards
Although there is near-universal recognition of the value in systematic weather and climate measurements, these measurements will have little value unless they conform to accepted standards. There is not a single source for standards for collecting weather and climate data nor a single standard that meets all needs. Measurement standards have been developed by the American Association of State Climatologists (AASC 1985), U.S. Environmental Protection Agency (EPA 1987), World Meteorological Organization (WMO 1983; 2005), Finklin and Fischer (1990), National Wildfire Coordinating Group (2004), and the RAWS program (Bureau of Land Management [BLM] 1997). Variations to these measurement standards also have been offered by instrument makers (e.g., Tanner 1990).

1.4.8. Who Makes the Measurements?
The lands under NPS stewardship provide many excellent locations to host the monitoring of climate by the NPS or other collaborators. These lands are largely protected from human development and other land changes that can impact observed climate records. Most park units historically have observed weather/climate elements as part of their overall mission. Many of these measurements come from station networks managed by other agencies, with observations taken or overseen by NPS personnel, in some cases, or by collaborators from the other agencies. National Park Service units that are small, lack sufficient resources, or lack sites presenting adequate exposure may benefit by utilizing weather/climate measurements collected from nearly stations.

2.0. Climate Background

The parks in the GULN represent a broad range of upland, freshwater, and coastal ecosystems, including the most extensive wetland areas in the U.S. These ecosystems are strongly influenced by climate characteristics (Twilley et al. 2001; Twilley and Rivera-Monroy 2005; Segura et al. 2005). Compared to other I&M networks, the GULN is uniquely vulnerable to potential sea level rises due to future climate changes, as these rises would inundate substantial tracts of valuable coastal wetlands, particularly in Louisiana (Penland and Ramsey 1990; Ning and Abdollahi 1999; Twilley et al. 2001).

It is essential that the GULN park units have an effective climate monitoring system to track climate changes and to aid in management decisions relating to these changes. These efforts are needed in order to support current vital sign monitoring activities within the park units of the GULN. In order to do this, however, it is essential to understand the climate characteristics of the GULN, as discussed in this chapter.

2.1. Climate and the GULN Environment

The GULN climate results from the interplay of regional factors, such as its latitude and the influence of nearby oceans, and global factors that include the El Niño Southern Oscillation (ENSO). As a result of substantial influences from the Gulf of Mexico and adjacent water bodies, the entire GULN experiences relatively warm conditions year round; however occasional cold air masses from the northern Pacific or the Arctic can bring freezing conditions (Twilley and Rivera-Monroy 2005). The westernmost portions of the GULN sub-region are semi-arid and conditions become more humid to the east. Precipitation throughout the network typically comes in the form of rain from winter and spring storm fronts, thunderstorms, and tropical storms and hurricanes in the summer and/or early fall (Twilley and Rivera-Monroy 2005).

The ENSO cycle plays a large role in the interannual variations of the GULN climate. El Niño years typically bring lower temperatures in winter and spring and increased winter precipitation throughout the GULN. During La Niña years, however, drought conditions can occur, such as those that occurred in the central and western Gulf Coast from 1998 to 2000. These drought periods can have significant negative consequences on GULN ecosystems, since many of these systems are very dependent on water availability (Mulholland et al. 1997).

Future climate changes may lead to more frequent drought conditions across much of the GULN (Twilley et al. 2001). Projected climate changes are expected to bring changes in coastal productivity due to variations in river runoff (Miller and Russel 1992; Justic et al. 1996). In both coastal and inland ecosystems, the future climate of the GULN may further facilitate the introduction of diseases and accelerated spread of non-native species (Bruce et al. 1995; Mulholland et al. 1997; Harcombe et al. 1998; Cooter et al. 2000). Exotic plant species introduced to the GULN have already had negative impacts on the region's ecosystems. An example is the Chinese tallow tree, which has become a major management issue in the coastal prairies of the GULN park units in south Texas (Bruce et al. 1995).

The ENSO pattern also has a strong influence on the number of Gulf Coast tropical storms and hurricanes (Gray 1984a; 1984b; Goldenberg and Shapiro 1996; Bove et al. 1998), which regularly make landfall along the Gulf Coast during the summer and fall months (Smith 1999; Lyons 2004). Hurricanes play a significant role in shaping the structure and characteristics of GULN ecosystems, particularly coastal systems (Stone et al. 1999; Twilley et al. 2001). Recent hurricanes such as Ivan (in 2004) and Katrina (in 2005) have had severe impacts on park units such as GUIS and have highlighted the vulnerability of coastal ecosystems. During La Niña events, the average number of hurricanes coming ashore in the Gulf of Mexico is typically higher than during El Niño or non-ENSO years (Bove et al. 1998). Although it is still yet uncertain if the intensity of land-falling hurricanes along the Gulf of Mexico is increasing (Bove et al. 1998; Henderson-Sellers et al. 1998; NAST 2001; Trenberth 2005), it is likely that with the current decreases in wetland areas across the GULN and potential sea level rises, future tropical storms and hurricanes will have an increasingly damaging affect on the GULN ecosystems.

Several of the management issues identified for the park units of the GULN (Segura et al. 2005) have impacts on local climate, and vice versa. Human impacts are apparent in varying degrees for all the park units of the GULN. These human influences have introduced disturbances and land-use heterogeneities that have introduced local- and regional-scale climate changes in the GULN. These land-use patterns adversely affect the ability of the plant and animal communities in the GULN to adapt to future climate changes and compete successfully with newly-established non-native species (Reid and Trexler 1992; Cooter et al. 2000).

2.2. Spatial Variability

The Gulf of Mexico influences strongly the climate characteristics of the GULN. Mean annual precipitation is greatest along and just inland of the east-central Gulf Coast. Park units in this zone, such as GUIS and JELA, generally receive 1600 mm or more of precipitation each year (Figure 2.1). This mean annual precipitation tends to decrease both inland and to the west. Vicksburg National Military Park (VICK) and much of the NATR receive between 1400 mm and 1600 mm of precipitation each year. Precipitation drops off drastically into east Texas, with the driest park units (PAAL, PAIS, and SAAN) receiving less than 800 mm of precipitation each year, on average. The seasonal timing of this precipitation varies greatly throughout the GULN (Figure 2.2). Along the western Gulf Coast, the wettest time of year tends to occur during a short time span in late summer and early fall (e.g., Figure 2.2a). Further east along the Gulf Coast, the entire summer period tends to be wet (e.g., Figure 2.2b). This differs significantly from inland locations, where precipitation is generally greatest in the winter and spring, with a dry season during the fall (e.g., Figure 2.2c).

Mean annual temperatures in the GULN (Figure 2.3) also tend to vary according to distance from the Gulf of Mexico, with park units along the Gulf Coast being warmest. Most of the GULN park units along the coast have mean annual temperatures between 18-20°C. The warmest park unit is PAAL, with mean annual temperatures just above 22°C. The coolest conditions are generally found along northern NATR, where mean annual temperatures are less than 12°C. This same temperature distribution is apparent in the map of mean January minimum temperatures for the GULN (Figure 2.4), with mild conditions along the coast and much colder conditions inland. The warmest park unit is again PAAL, where January minimum temperatures generally do not get below 8°C. However, these same temperatures regularly get below -4°C along northern portions of NATR. In fact, January temperatures have approached -20°C along northern portions of NATR during severe cold snaps. Summer temperatures (e.g. Figure 2.5) vary largely along an

Figure 2.1. Mean annual precipitation, 1961-1990, for the GULN.

11

a)

b)

c)

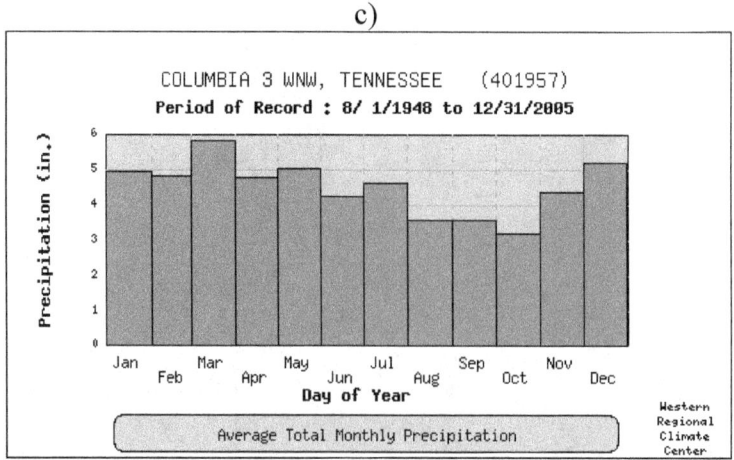

Figure 2.2. Mean monthly precipitation at selected stations in the GULN. Port Isabel (a) is near PAAL, Abbeville (b) is near JELA, and Columbia 3 WNW (c) is near the northern end of NATR.

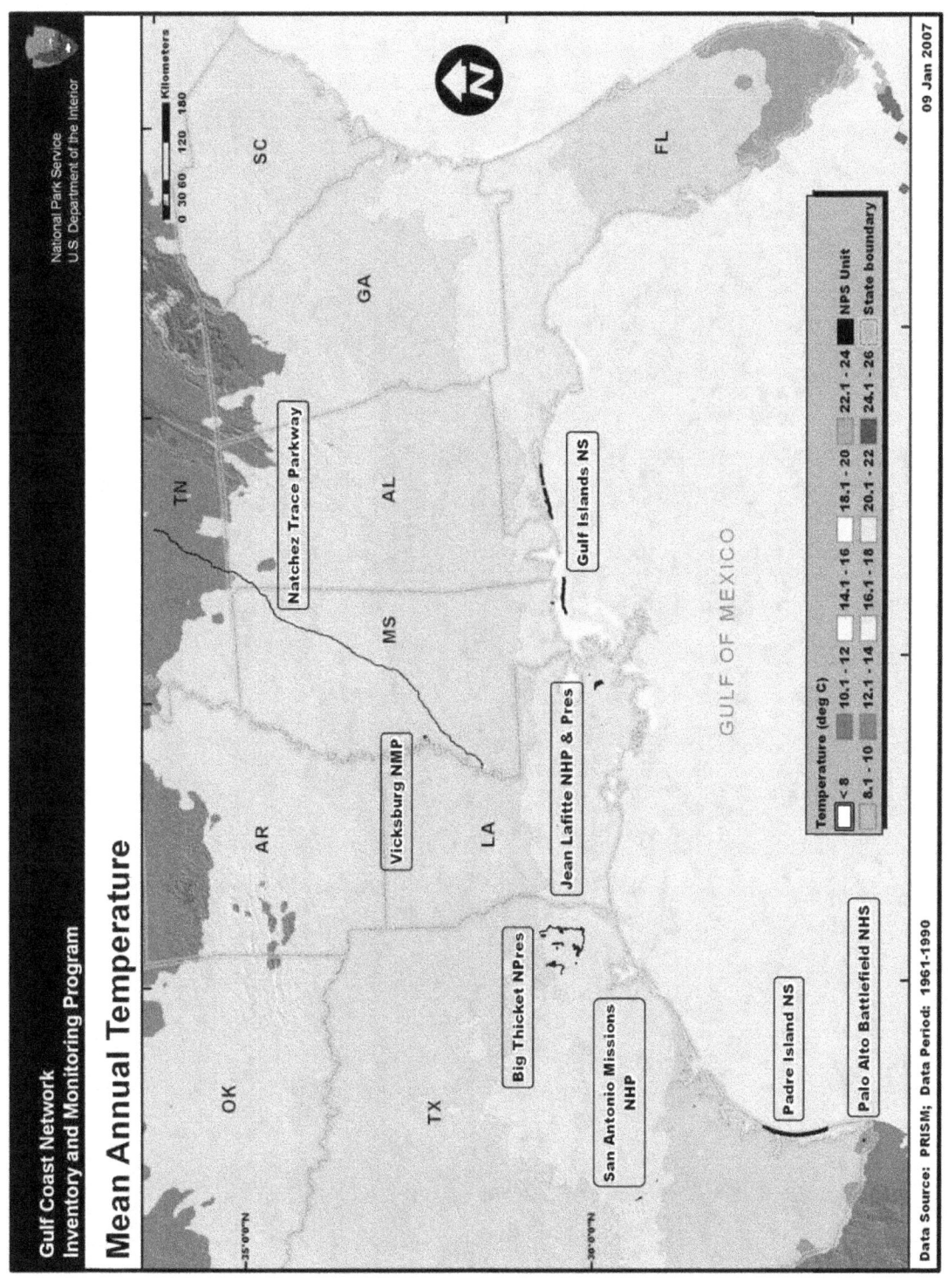

Figure 2.3. Mean annual temperature, 1961-1990, for the GULN.

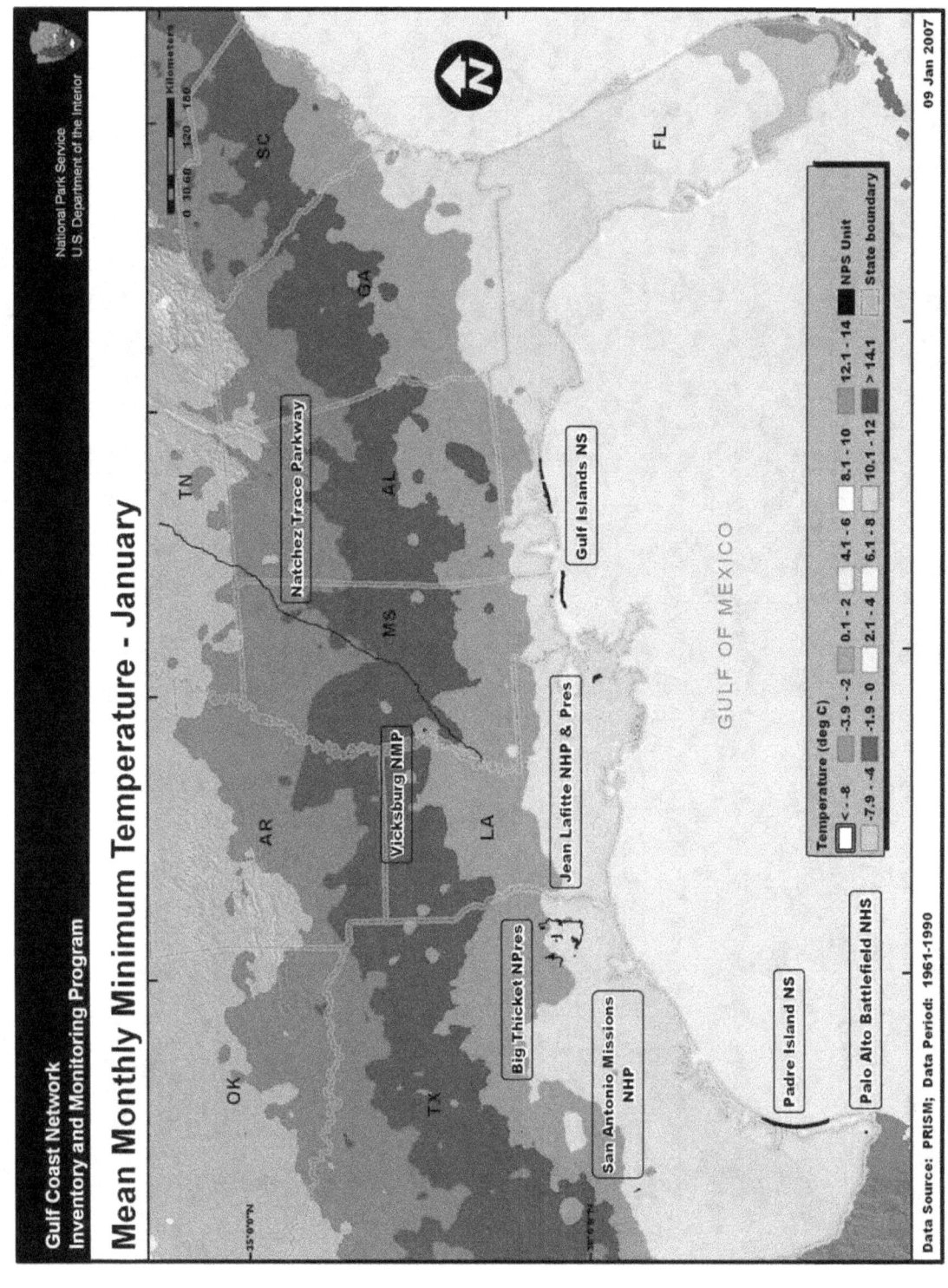

Figure 2.4. Mean January minimum temperature, 1961-1990, for the GULN.

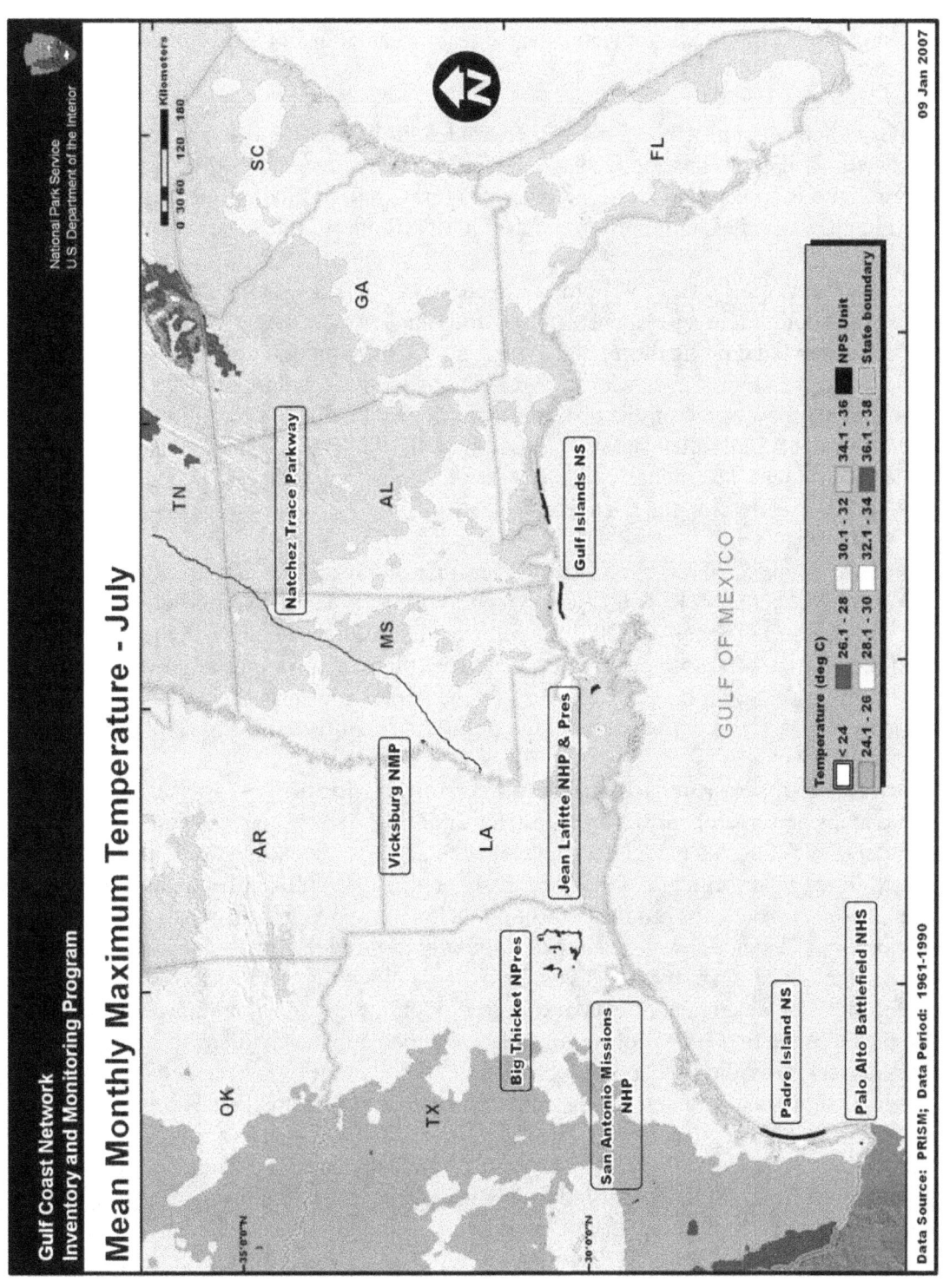

Figure 2.5. Mean July maximum temperature, 1961-1990, for the GULN.

east-west gradient across the GULN. Due to moderating effects from the Gulf of Mexico, July maximum temperatures along coastal park units are generally under 32°C. However, park units further inland see maximum temperatures that are a couple of degrees higher. The warmest conditions are in Texas, with mean July maximum temperatures at SAAN between 34-36°C. Summer temperatures in the SAAN vicinity have reached as high as 45°C.

2.3. Temporal Variability

Most studies indicate that precipitation has increased slightly over the last century for much of the southeastern U.S., including the GULN (NAST 2001; Twilley et al. 2001). No obvious precipitation trend is apparent in western GULN (Figure 2.6a), but increasing precipitation trends are evident in central and eastern portions of the GULN (Figures 2.6b; 2.6c).

Temperature patterns for the GULN (Figure 2.7) are quite variable over the past century and in some cases show cooling, in agreement with previous studies (see NAST 2001; Twilley et al. 2001). After substantial cooling during the 1960s and 1970s, temperatures in the GULN have warmed steadily, particularly in central and western portions of the network (see Figures 2.7a; 2.7b). It is not clear how much of this observed pattern may be due to discontinuities in temperature records at individual stations, caused by artificial changes such as stations moves. These patterns highlight the emphasis on measurement consistency that is needed in order to properly detect long-term climatic changes.

As previously mentioned, ENSO cycles strongly influence interannual climate variability in the GULN. Warm ENSO phases (El Niño events) tend to bring cooler and wetter winter conditions across the southeastern U.S. (NAST 2001; Twilley et al. 2001), particularly in the southern portions of the GULN. Increased occurrences of severe thunderstorms are also evident in the GULN during warm ENSO phases, particularly in the winter and spring months. Hurricanes and other tropical storm activity tend to decrease in the GULN during warm ENSO phases.

2.4. Parameter Regression on Independent Slopes Model

The climate maps presented here were generated using the Parameter Regression on Independent Slopes Model (PRISM). This model was developed to address the extreme spatial and elevation gradients exhibited by the climate of the U.S. (Daly et al. 1994; 2002; Gibson et al. 2002; Doggett et al. 2004). The maps produced through PRISM have undergone rigorous evaluation for the entire U.S. This model was developed originally to provide climate information at scales matching available land-cover maps to assist in ecologic modeling. The PRISM technique accounts for the scale-dependent effects of topography on mean values of climate elements. Elevation provides the first-order constraint for the mapped climate fields, with slope and orientation (aspect) providing second-order constraints. The model has been enhanced gradually to address inversions, coast/land gradients, and climate patterns in small-scale trapping basins. Monthly climate fields are generated by PRISM to account for seasonal variations in elevation gradients in climate elements. These monthly climate fields then can be combined into seasonal and annual climate fields. Since PRISM maps are grid maps, they do not replicate point values but rather, for a given grid cell, represent the grid-cell average of the climate variable in question at the average elevation for that cell. The model relies on observed surface and upper-air measurements to estimate spatial climate fields.

a)

b)

c)

Figure 2.6. Precipitation time series, 1895-2005, for selected regions in the GULN. These include twelve-month precipitation (ending in December) (red), 10-year running mean (blue), mean (green), and plus/minus one standard deviation (green dotted). Locations include south-central Texas (a), southeastern Louisiana (b), and central Mississippi (c).

17

a)

b)

c)

Figure 2.7. Temperature time series, 1895-2005, for selected regions in the GULN. These include twelve-month average temperature (ending in December) (red), 10-year running mean (blue), mean (green), and plus/minus one standard deviation (green dotted). Locations include south-central Texas (a), southeastern Louisiana (b), and central Mississippi (c).

18

3.0. Methods

Having discussed the climatic characteristics of the GULN, we now present the procedures that were used to obtain information for weather/climate stations within the GULN. This information was obtained from various sources, as mentioned in the following paragraphs. Retrieval of station metadata constituted a major component of this work.

3.1. Metadata Retrieval

A key component of station inventories is determining the kinds of observations that have been conducted over time, by whom, and in what manner; when each type of observation began and ended; and whether these observations are still being conducted. Metadata about the observational process (Table 3.1) generally consist of a series of vignettes that apply to time intervals and, therefore, constitute a *history* rather than a single snapshot. An expanded list of relevant metadata fields for this inventory is provided in Appendix E. This report has relied on metadata records from three sources: (a) Western Regional Climate Center (WRCC), (b) NPS personnel, and (c) other knowledgeable personnel, such as state climate office staff.

The initial metadata sources for this report were stored at WRCC. This regional climate center (RCC) acts as a working repository of many western climate records, including the main networks outlined in this section. The WRCC conducts live and periodic data collection (ingests) from all major national and western weather/climate networks. These networks include the COOP network, the Surface Airways Observation network (SAO) operated by NWS and the Federal Aviation Administration (FAA), the interagency RAWS network, and various smaller networks. The WRCC is expanding its capability to ingest information from other networks as resources permit and usefulness dictates. This center has relied heavily on historic archives (in many cases supplemented with live ingests) to assess the quantity (not necessarily quality) of data available for NPS I&M network applications.

The primary source of metadata at WRCC is the Applied Climate Information System (ACIS), a joint effort among RCCs and other NOAA entities. Metadata for GULN weather/climate stations identified from the ACIS database are available in file "GULN_from_ACIS.tar.gz" (see Appendix F). Historic metadata pertaining to major climate- and weather-observing systems in the U.S. are stored in ACIS where metadata are linked to the observed data. A distributed system, ACIS is synchronized among the RCCs. Mainstream software is utilized, including Postgress, Python™, and Java™ programming languages; CORBA®-compliant network software; and industry-standard, nonproprietary hardware and software. Metadata and data for all major national climate and weather networks have been entered into the ACIS database. For this project, the available metadata from many smaller networks also have been entered but in most cases the actual data have not yet been entered. Data sets are in the NetCDF (Network Common Data Form) format, but the design allows for integration with legacy systems, including non-NetCDF files (used at WRCC) and additional metadata (added for this project). The ACIS also supports a suite of products to visualize or summarize data from these data sets. National climate-monitoring maps are updated daily using the ACIS data feed. The developmental phases of ACIS have utilized metadata supplied by the NCDC and NWS with many tens of thousands of entries, screened as well as possible for duplications, mistakes, and omissions.

Table 3.1. Primary metadata fields for GULN weather/climate stations. Explanations are provided as appropriate.

Metadata Field	Notes
Station name	Station name associated with network listed in "Climate Network."
Latitude	Numerical value (units: see coordinate units).
Longitude	Numerical value (units: see coordinate units).
Coordinate units	Latitude/longitude (units: decimal degrees, degree-minute-second, etc.).
Datum	Datum used as basis for coordinates: WGS 84, NAD 83, etc.
Elevation	Elevation of station above mean sea level (m).
Slope	Slope of ground surface below station (degrees).
Aspect	Azimuth that ground surface below station faces.
Climate division	NOAA climate division where station is located. Climate divisions are NOAA-specified zones sharing similar climate and hydrology characteristics.
Country	Country where station is located.
State	State where station is located.
County	County where station is located.
Weather/climate network	Primary weather/climate network the station belongs to (RAWS, Clean Air Status and Trends Network [CASTNet], etc.).
NPS unit code	Four-letter code identifying park unit where station resides.
NPS unit name	Full name of park unit.
NPS unit type	National park, national monument, etc.
UTM zone	If UTM is the only coordinate system available.
Location notes	Useful information not already included in "station narrative."
Climate variables	Temperature, precipitation, etc.
Installation date	Date of station installation.
Removal date	Date of station removal.
Station photograph	Digital image of station.
Photograph date	Date photograph was taken.
Photographer	Name of person who took the photograph.
Station narrative	Anything related to general site description; may include site exposure, characteristics of surrounding vegetation, driving directions, etc.
Contact name	Name of the person involved with station operation.
Organization	Group or agency affiliation of contact person.
Contact type	Designation that identifies contact person as the station owner, observer, maintenance person, data manager, etc.
Position/job title	Official position/job title of contact person.
Address	Address of contact person.
E-mail address	E-mail address of contact person.
Phone	Phone number of contact person (and extension if available).
Contact notes	Other information needed to reach contact person.

In addition to obtaining GULN weather/climate station metadata from ACIS, metadata were obtained from NPS staff at the GULN office in Lafayette, Louisiana. The metadata provided from the GULN office are available in file "GULN_NPS.tar.gz." Most of the stations noted by

GULN staff are already accounted for in ACIS. We have also relied on information supplied at various times in the past by the BLM, NPS, NCDC, and NWS.

Two types of information have been used to complete the GULN climate station inventory.

- Station inventories: Information about observational procedures, latitude/longitude, elevation, measured elements, measurement frequency, sensor types, exposures, ground cover and vegetation, data-processing details, network, purpose, and managing individual or agency, etc.

- Data inventories: Information about measured data values including completeness, seasonality, data gaps, representation of missing data, flagging systems, how special circumstances in the data record are denoted, etc.

This is not a straightforward process. Extensive searches are typically required to develop historic station and data inventories. Both types of inventories frequently contain information gaps and often rely on tacit and unrealistic assumptions. Sources of information for these inventories frequently are difficult to recover or are undocumented and unreliable. In many cases, the actual weather/climate data available from different sources are not linked directly to metadata records. To the extent that actual data can be acquired (rather than just metadata), it is possible to cross-check these records and perform additional assessments based on the amount and completeness of the data.

Certain types of weather/climate networks that possess any of the following attributes have not been considered for inclusion in the inventory:

- Private networks with proprietary access and/or inability to obtain or provide sufficient metadata.
- Private weather enthusiasts (often with high-quality data) whose metadata are not available and whose data are not readily accessible.
- Unofficial observers supplying data to the NWS (lack of access to current data and historic archives; lack of metadata).
- Networks having no available historic data.
- Networks having poor-quality metadata.
- Networks having poor access to metadata.
- Real-time networks having poor access to real-time data.

Previous inventory efforts at WRCC have shown that for the weather networks identified in the preceding list, in light of the need for quality data to track weather and climate, the resources required and difficulty encountered in obtaining metadata or data are prohibitively large.

3.2. Criteria for Locating Stations

To identify stations for each park unit in the GULN, we selected all weather and climate stations, past and present, which were located inside GULN park units or within 30 km of a GULN park-unit boundary. We selected a 30-km buffer in order to ensure the inclusion of a sufficient number of both manual and automated stations in and near the park units in the GULN, while at the same time keeping the number of identified stations at a reasonable level.

The station locator maps presented in Chapter 4 were designed to show clearly the spatial distributions of all major weather/climate station networks in GULN. We recognize that other mapping formats may be more suitable for other specific needs.

4.0. Station Inventory

An objective of this report is to show the locations of weather/climate stations for the GULN region in relation to the boundaries of the NPS park units within the GULN. A station does not have to be within park boundaries to provide useful data and information for a park unit.

4.1. Climate and Weather Networks

Most stations in the GULN region are associated with at least one of 13 weather/climate networks (Table 4.1). Brief descriptions of each weather/climate network are provided below (see Appendix G for greater detail).

Table 4.1. Weather/climate networks represented within the GULN.

Acronym	Name
CASTNet	Clean Air Status and Trends Network
COOP	NWS Cooperative Observer Program
CRN	NOAA Climate Reference Network
CWOP	Citizen Weather Observer Program
GPMP	Gaseous Pollutant Monitoring Program
GPS-MET	NOAA ground-based GPS meteorology network
MEXICO	Mexico weather/climate stations
NADP	National Atmospheric Deposition Program
POMS	Portable Ozone Monitoring System network
RAWS	Remote Automated Weather Station network
SAO	NWS/FAA Surface Airways Observation network
SCAN	Soil Climate Analysis Network
WX4U	Weather For You network

4.1.1. Clean Air Status and Trends Network (CASTNet)

CASTNet is primarily an air-quality monitoring network managed by the EPA. Standard hourly weather and climate elements are measured and include temperature, wind, humidity, solar radiation, soil temperature, and sometimes moisture. These elements are intended to support interpretation of air-quality parameters that also are measured at CASTNet sites. Data records at CASTNet sites are generally one–two decades in length.

4.1.2. NWS Cooperative Observer Program (COOP)

The COOP network has been a foundation of the U.S. climate program for decades and continues to play an important role. Manual measurements are made by volunteers and consist of daily maximum and minimum temperatures, observation-time temperature, daily precipitation, daily snowfall, and snow depth. When blended with NWS measurements, the data set is known as SOD, or "Summary of the Day." The quality of data from COOP sites ranges from excellent to modest.

4.1.3. NOAA Climate Reference Network (CRN)

The CRN is intended as a reference network for the U.S. that meets the requirements of the Global Climate Observing System. Up to 115 CRN sites are planned for installation, but the actual number of installed sites will depend on available funding. Standard meteorological elements are measured. CRN data are used in operational climate-monitoring activities and to place current climate patterns in historic perspective.

4.1.4. Citizen Weather Observer Program (CWOP)

The CWOP network consists primarily of automated weather stations operated by private citizens who have either an Internet connection and/or a wireless Ham radio setup. Data from CWOP stations are specifically intended for use in research, education, and homeland security activities. Although meteorological elements such as temperature, precipitation, and wind are measured at all CWOP stations, station characteristics do vary, including sensor types and site exposure.

4.1.5. Gaseous Pollutant Monitoring Program (GPMP)

The GPMP network measures hourly meteorological data in support of pollutant monitoring activities. Measured elements include temperature, precipitation, humidity, wind, solar radiation, and surface wetness. These data are generally of high quality, with records extending up to 1-2 decades in length.

4.1.6. NOAA Ground-Based GPS Meteorology (GPS-MET) Network

The GPS-MET network is the first network of its kind dedicated to GPS (Global Positioning System) meteorology (see Duan et al. 1996). GPS meteorology utilizes the radio signals broadcast by the satellite Global Positioning System for atmospheric remote sensing. GPS meteorology applications have evolved along two paths: ground-based (Bevis et al. 1992) and space-based (Yuan et al. 1993). For more information, please see Appendix G. The stations identified in this inventory are all ground-based. The GPS-MET network was developed in response to the need for improved moisture observations to support weather forecasting, climate monitoring, and other research activities. The primary goals of this network are to measure atmospheric water vapor using ground-based GPS receivers, facilitate the operational use of these data, and encourage usage of GPS meteorology for atmospheric research and other applications. GPS-MET is a collaboration between NOAA and several other governmental and university organizations and institutions. Ancillary meteorological observations at GPS-MET stations include temperature, relative humidity, and pressure.

4.1.7. Mexico Weather/Climate Stations (MEXICO)

These include various automated weather/climate station networks from Mexico. The National Meteorological Services (Servicio Meteorológico Nacional) operates many of these stations, including airport sites. The data measured at these sites generally include temperature, precipitation, humidity, wind, and barometric pressure.

4.1.8. National Atmospheric Deposition Program (NADP)

The purpose of the NADP network is to monitor primarily wet deposition at selected sites around the U.S. and its territories. The network is a collaborative effort among several agencies including the U.S. Geological Survey (USGS) and USDA. This network includes the Mercury

Deposition Network (MDN). Precipitation is the primary climate parameter measured at NADP sites.

4.1.9. Portable Ozone Monitoring System (POMS) Network
The POMS network is operated by the NPS Air Resources Division. Sites are intended primarily for summer, short-term (1-5 years) monitoring of near-surface atmospheric ozone levels in remote locations. Measured meteorological elements include temperature, precipitation, wind, relative humidity, and solar radiation.

4.1.10. Remote Automated Weather Station (RAWS) Network
The RAWS network is administered through many land management agencies, particularly the BLM and the Forest Service. Hourly meteorology elements are measured and include temperature, wind, humidity, solar radiation, barometric pressure, fuel temperature, and precipitation (when temperatures are above freezing). The fire community is the primary client for RAWS data. These sites are remote and data typically are transmitted via GOES (Geostationary Operational Environmental Satellite). Some sites operate all winter. Most data records for RAWS sites began during or after the mid-1980s.

4.1.11. NWS/FAA Surface Airways Observation (SAO) Network
These stations are located usually at major airports and military bases. Almost all SAO sites are automated. The hourly data measured at these sites include temperature, precipitation, humidity, wind, pressure, sky cover, ceiling, visibility, and current weather. Most data records begin during or after the 1940s, and these data are generally of high quality.

4.1.12. USDA/NRCS Soil Climate Analysis Network (SCAN)
The SCAN network is administered by NRCS and is intended to be a comprehensive nationwide soil moisture and climate information system to be used in supporting natural resource assessments and other conservation activities. These stations are usually located in the agricultural areas of the U.S. All SCAN sites are automated. The parameters measured at these sites include air temperature, precipitation, humidity, wind, pressure, solar radiation, snow depth, and snow water content.

4.1.13. Weather For You Network (WX4U)
The WX4U network is a nationwide collection of weather stations run by local observers. Data quality varies with site. Standard meteorological elements are measured and usually include temperature, precipitation, wind, and humidity.

4.1.14. Weather Bureau Army Navy (WBAN)
This is a station identification system rather than a true weather/climate network. Stations identified with WBAN are largely historical stations that reported meteorological observations on the WBAN weather observation forms that were common during the early and middle parts of the twentieth century. The use of WBAN numbers to identify stations was one of the first attempts in the U.S. to use a coordinated station numbering scheme between several weather station networks, such as the SAO and COOP networks.

4.1.15. Other Networks

In addition to the major networks mentioned above, there are various networks that are operated for specific purposes by specific organizations or governmental agencies or scientific research projects, which could be present within GULN but have not been identified in this report. Some of the commonly used networks include the following:

- NOAA upper-air stations
- Federal and state departments of transportation
- U.S. Department of Energy Surface Radiation Budget Network (Surfrad)
- USGS hydrologic stations
- Park-specific-monitoring networks and stations
- Other research or project networks having many possible owners

4.2. Station Locations

The major weather/climate networks in the GULN (discussed in Section 4.1) have at most several stations that are inside each park unit (Table 4.2). Gulf Islands National Seashore (GUIS) has the greatest number of stations inside park boundaries (six).

Table 4.2. Number of stations within or nearby GULN park units. Numbers are listed by park unit and by weather/climate network. Figures in parentheses indicate the numbers of stations within park boundaries.

Network	BITH	GUIS	JELA	NATR	PAAL	PAIS	SAAN	VICK
CASTNet	1(0)	0(0)	0(0)	0(0)	0(0)	0(0)	0(0)	0(0)
COOP	37(1)	33(1)	65(1)	160(2)	10(0)	10(1)	20(0)	15(1)
CRN	0(0)	0(0)	1(0)	0(0)	0(0)	0(0)	0(0)	0(0)
CWOP	2(0)	21(0)	14(0)	25(0)	2(0)	2(0)	9(0)	0(0)
GPMP	1(1)	0(0)	0(0)	0(0)	0(0)	0(0)	0(0)	0(0)
GPS-MET	1(0)	0(0)	2(0)	2(0)	0(0)	1(0)	1(0)	1(0)
MEXICO	0(0)	0(0)	0(0)	0(0)	1(0)	0(0)	0(0)	0(0)
NADP	0(0)	0(0)	0(0)	1(0)	0(0)	1(0)	0(0)	0(0)
POMS	0(0)	1(1)	0(0)	0(0)	0(0)	1(1)	0(0)	0(0)
RAWS	4(1)	4(1)	3(0)	7(1)	1(0)	0(0)	0(0)	1(1)
SAO	2(0)	17(1)	10(0)	8(0)	5(0)	4(0)	6(0)	2(0)
SCAN	0(0)	1(0)	0(0)	1(0)	0(0)	0(0)	0(0)	0(0)
WX4U	0(0)	3(1)	0(0)	3(0)	0(0)	0(0)	2(0)	0(0)
Other	1(0)	12(1)	2(0)	3(0)	1(0)	0(0)	1(0)	0(0)
Total	49(3)	92(6)	97(1)	210(3)	20(0)	19(2)	39(0)	19(2)

Lists of stations have been compiled for the GULN. A station does not have to be within the boundaries to provide useful data and information regarding the park unit in question. Some might be physically *within* the administrative or political boundaries, whereas others might be just outside, or even some distance away, but would be *nearby* in behavior and representativeness. What constitutes "useful" and "representative" are also significant questions, whose answers can vary according to application, type of element, period of record, procedural or methodological observation conventions, and the like.

4.2.1. South Texas

No weather/climate stations were identified within PAAL. Four active COOP stations are located within 30 km of PAAL (Table 4.3). The longest record of these stations comes from "Port Isabel," which is located 15 km east of PAAL (Figure 4.1) and started taking measurements in 1896. This station's data record has at least two significant data gaps, one gap occurring from October 1969 to March 1975 and the other gap occurring from June 1983 to January 1984. The COOP station "Brownsville S. Padre I. Intl. Arpt.," 10 km south of PAAL, also has a data record extending back to the 1890s. This data record is very complete. A third long-term climate record comes from the COOP station "Harlingen," 26 km northwest of PAAL. This station has been active since 1911. The data record at "Harlingen" is largely complete with the exception of a data gap from August 1971 to February 1972.

Table 4.3. Weather/climate stations for the GULN park units in south Texas. Stations inside park units and within 30 km of the park unit boundaries are included. Missing entries are indicated by "M".

Name	Lat.	Lon.	Elev. (m)	Network	Start	End	In Park?
Palo Alto Battlefield National Historic Site – PAAL							
Bay View	26.133	-97.400	6	COOP	7/1/1947	7/31/1974	No
Brownsville	25.901	-97.504	5	COOP	11/1/1906	12/16/2003	No
Brownsville S. Padre I. Intl. Arpt.	25.914	-97.423	7	COOP	12/1/1898	Present	No
Brownsville WBO	25.917	-97.467	27	COOP	5/1/1877	12/31/1942	No
Harlingen	26.203	-97.673	12	COOP	5/1/1911	Present	No
Los Fresnos	26.067	-97.483	9	COOP	11/1/1961	3/24/1966	No
Port Isabel	26.094	-97.309	5	COOP	2/22/1896	Present	No
Port Isabel Lightboat	26.067	-97.167	3	COOP	M	Present	No
San Benito	26.133	-97.633	12	COOP	3/1/1920	6/30/1975	No
San Benito Filter Plant	26.133	-97.633	12	COOP	7/1/1947	5/31/1950	No
CW4827 S. Padre Island	26.099	-97.168	2	CWOP	M	Present	No
KI0G-3 Port Isabel	26.068	-97.205	3	CWOP	M	Present	No
Matamoros International	25.767	-97.533	8	MEXICO	M	Present	No
Laguna Atascosa	26.228	-97.348	8	RAWS	2/1/2002	Present	No
Brownsville S. Padre I. Intl. Arpt.	25.914	-97.423	7	SAO	12/1/1898	Present	No
Harlingen Harvey Richards Fld.	26.200	-97.683	13	SAO	7/1/1960	12/21/1967	No
Harlingen Rio Grande Valley In.	26.228	-97.654	10	SAO	3/1/1942	Present	No
Port Isabel Cameron Co. Arpt.	26.166	-97.346	6	SAO	11/1/1957	Present	No
Port Isabel Lightboat	26.067	-97.167	3	SAO	M	Present	No
Fort Brown ASC	25.883	-97.550	12	WBAN	1/1/1878	12/31/1929	No
Padre Island National Seashore – PAIS							
Padre Island Natl. Sea.	27.447	-97.297	3	COOP	4/1/1959	Present	Yes
Malaquite Visitor Center	27.427	-97.298	6	POMS	5/1/2005	Present	Yes
Armstrong 4 SE	26.834	-97.708	8	COOP	1/5/2002	Present	No
Brighton	27.650	-97.300	3	COOP	8/1/1892	1/31/1920	No
Chapman Ranch	27.589	-97.455	8	COOP	3/1/1959	6/1/2003	No

Name	Lat.	Lon.	Elev. (m)	Network	Start	End	In Park?
Corpus Christi Botanical Gardens	27.653	-97.407	5	COOP	10/1/2003	Present	No
Corpus Christi Padre	27.583	-97.217	3	COOP	M	6/30/1967	No
Flour Bluff	27.600	-97.283	3	COOP	9/1/1988	2/1/1999	No
Port Mansfield	26.558	-97.426	3	COOP	2/1/1958	Present	No
San Perlita	26.500	-97.600	6	COOP	7/1/1947	5/31/1950	No
Sarita 7 E	27.217	-97.696	12	COOP	5/1/1899	Present	No
CW4204 Corpus Christi	27.652	-97.297	5	CWOP	M	Present	No
CW5772 Corpus Christi	27.598	-97.235	10	CWOP	M	Present	No
Corpus Christi	27.740	-97.440	16	GPS-MET	M	Present	No
Texas A&M-Corpus Christi	27.713	-97.329	5	NADP	1/2/2002	Present	No
Cabaniss Field NALF	27.700	-97.433	10	SAO	M	Present	No
Corpus Christi Cabaniss Field	27.683	-97.450	14	SAO	1/1/1949	8/31/1973	No
Corpus Christi NAS	27.683	-97.283	6	SAO	4/1/1941	Present	No
Port Mansfield	26.558	-97.426	3	SAO	2/1/1958	Present	No

San Antonio Missions National Historical Park – SAAN

Name	Lat.	Lon.	Elev. (m)	Network	Start	End	In Park?
Cibolo Creek	29.017	-97.933	95	COOP	5/2/1944	9/29/1983	No
Coy City 4 WNW	28.850	-98.100	143	COOP	10/1/1957	6/30/1961	No
Elmendorf	29.417	-98.333	214	COOP	5/1/1916	Present	No
Falls City 7 WSW	28.961	-98.110	105	COOP	8/1/1946	Present	No
Floresville	29.132	-98.160	122	COOP	6/1/1916	Present	No
Floresville 2 ESE	29.133	-98.100	125	COOP	2/1/1980	1/31/1982	No
Floresville 7 SSW	29.050	-98.217	143	COOP	2/1/1982	2/20/1986	No
La Vernia	29.367	-98.100	146	COOP	8/1/1941	5/31/1951	No
McCoy	28.861	-98.347	92	COOP	7/1/1961	8/15/2002	No
Randolph AFB	29.544	-98.274	232	COOP	4/1/1935	Present	No
San Antonio	29.450	-98.467	223	COOP	5/1/1876	12/31/1940	No
San Antonio 8 NNE	29.525	-98.454	240	COOP	12/1/1996	Present	No
San Antonio Intl. Arpt.	29.533	-98.470	247	COOP	7/1/1933	Present	No
San Antonio Kelly Field AFB	29.383	-98.583	208	COOP	12/1/1918	Present	No
San Antonio Nursery	29.300	-98.467	180	COOP	1/1/1893	9/30/1968	No
San Antonio Police Stn.	29.422	-98.497	187	COOP	6/15/2001	Present	No
San Antonio Stinson Municipal	29.339	-98.472	176	COOP	1/1/1941	Present	No
San Antonio/Seaworld	29.451	-98.703	287	COOP	6/1/1988	Present	No
Stockdale 4 N	29.288	-97.967	145	COOP	12/1/1940	Present	No
Sutherland Springs	29.283	-98.050	0	COOP	M	Present	No
CW0370 St. Hedwig	29.392	-98.209	176	CWOP	M	Present	No
CW0485 San Antonio	29.637	-98.445	344	CWOP	M	Present	No
CW1475 San Antonio	29.455	-98.539	210	CWOP	M	Present	No
CW1627 San Antonio	29.640	-98.497	360	CWOP	M	Present	No
CW2048 San Antonio	29.598	-98.528	305	CWOP	M	Present	No
CW4124 San Antonio	29.599	-98.375	308	CWOP	M	Present	No
CW5144 Schertz	29.578	-98.266	236	CWOP	M	Present	No
K5ZZT-5 San Antonio	29.553	-98.625	275	CWOP	M	Present	No

Name	Lat.	Lon.	Elev. (m)	Network	Start	End	In Park?
WA5FSR St. Hedwig	29.392	-98.209	176	CWOP	M	Present	No
San Antonio	29.540	-98.420	254	GPS-MET	M	Present	No
Randolph AFB	29.544	-98.274	232	SAO	4/1/1935	Present	No
San Antonio Brooks AFB	29.350	-98.450	182	SAO	11/1/1947	6/30/1960	No
San Antonio Intl. Arpt.	29.533	-98.470	247	SAO	7/1/1933	Present	No
San Antonio Kelly Field AFB	29.383	-98.583	208	SAO	12/1/1918	Present	No
San Antonio Lackland	29.000	-98.000	0	SAO	10/1/1951	1/31/1953	No
San Antonio Stinson Municipal	29.339	-98.472	176	SAO	1/1/1941	Present	No
Fort Sam Houston AAF	29.450	-98.467	232	WBAN	11/1/1933	12/31/1937	No
Northwest Crossing San Antonio	29.510	-98.680	278	WX4U	M	Present	No
San Antonio	29.544	-98.504	268	WX4U	M	Present	No

Several stations provide near-real-time weather data within 30 km of PAAL (Table 4.3), including a weather station in Mexico, 27 km south of PAAL (Matamoros International; see Figure 4.1). Two CWOP stations provide near-real-time data, one on South Padre Island and the other at Port Isabel. The RAWS station "Laguna Atascosa" is 23 km northeast of PAAL at Laguna Atascosa National Wildlife Refuge. Several active SAO sites provide near-real-time weather data within 30 km of PAAL. The most reliable source of near-real-time data is likely the SAO station "Brownsville S. Padre I. Intl. Arpt.," 10 km south of PAAL.

We identified two stations within PAIS (Table 4.3). Both of these stations are active currently. The COOP station "Padre Island Natl. Sea." has been active since 1959, while the POMS station "Malaquite Visitor Center" has been operating since 2005.

Of the nine COOP stations we identified within 30 km of PAIS, four are active currently (Table 4.3). The COOP station "Sarita 7 E" has the longest data record of these active sites (1899-present). This station, located 29 km west of PAIS, measured only precipitation until November 2004, when temperature observations began as well. The next longest record we identified is found at the COOP station "Port Mansfield," which is 10 km west of the south end of PAIS and has been active since 1958. The data record at "Port Mansfield" is largely complete.

The primary sources of near-real-time weather data for PAIS are located in or near Corpus Christi, Texas. Two of the active SAO stations we have identified are located in this area, 15-20 km northwest of PAIS (Figure 4.1). The remaining active SAO station, "Port Mansfield," is 10 km west of the south end of PAIS. Two CWOP stations and one NADP station are located in or near Corpus Christi (Table 4.3).

No weather/climate stations were identified within SAAN (Table 4.3; Figure 4.1). However, at least 12 active COOP stations are located within 30 km of SAAN. The closest active COOP station is "San Antonio Stinson Municipal," located less than one kilometer away from SAAN units in south San Antonio. This station has a data record going back to 1941. The longest record of these stations is at "Elmendorf" (1916-present), although the quality of this data record is

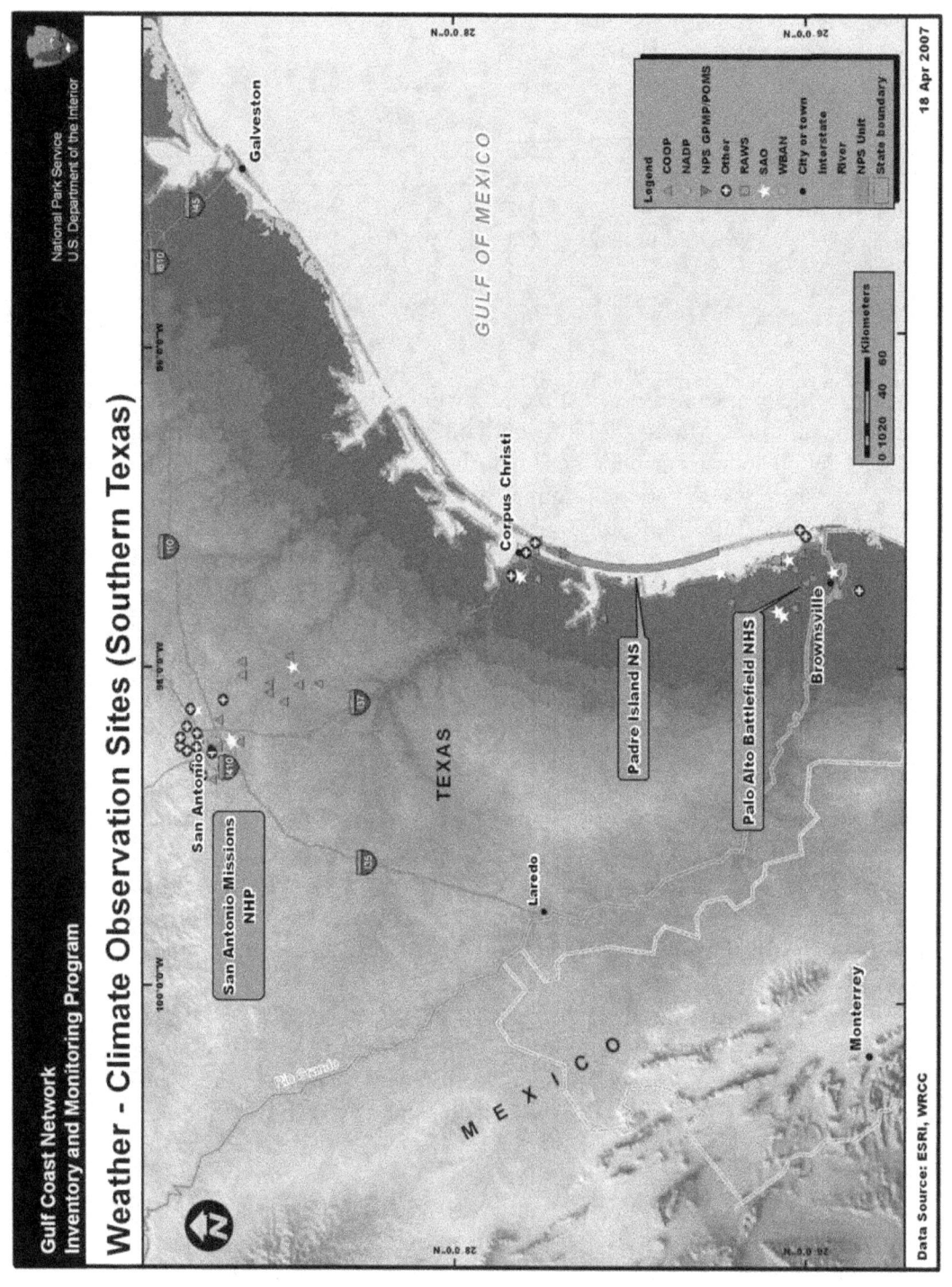

Figure 4.1. Station locations for the GULN park units in south Texas.

30

uncertain. Another long-term data record extending back to 1916 is available from the COOP station "Floresville," located 4 km from SAAN in southeast San Antonio. This station's data record is largely complete, although temperatures have only been measured there since September 1962. The COOP station "San Antonio Kelly Field AFB," 8 km from SAAN in southwest San Antonio, has a data record starting in 1918 but the quality of this data record is uncertain. The most reliable data record may come from the COOP station "San Antonio Intl. Arpt.," which is 16 km from SAAN in north-central San Antonio and has been making observations since 1933.

The primary sources of near-real-time weather data outside of SAAN are SAO stations in the San Antonio area (Figure 4.1). The four active SAO stations we identified for SAAN (Table 4.3) are also co-located with COOP stations. We have identified ten CWOP stations and two WX4U stations that also provide near-real-time weather data within 30 km of SAAN.

4.2.2. East Texas and Gulf Coast
Three stations were identified within BITH (Table 4.4), one of which is active currently. The active station is a RAWS station (Southern Rough) that provides near-real-time data in the Turkey Creek Unit of BITH. The remaining two stations are historical stations. A COOP station (Beaumont Bunns Bluff) was located in the Beaumont unit of BITH, while a GPMP station (Big Thicket) was located in the Turkey Creek unit of BITH.

Table 4.4. Weather/climate stations for GULN park units in east Texas and the Gulf Coast states. Stations inside park units and within 30 km of the park unit boundaries are included. Missing entries are indicated by "M".

Name	Lat.	Lon.	Elev. (m)	Network	Start	End	In Park?
Big Thicket National Preserve – BITH							
Beaumont Bunns Bluff	30.167	-94.117	0	COOP	12/1/1967	4/30/1973	Yes
Big Thicket	30.544	-94.346	32	GPMP	11/1/1985	1/31/1992	Yes
Southern Rough	30.540	-94.341	30	RAWS	3/1/1999	Present	Yes
Alabama-Coushatta	30.421	-94.404	0	CASTNet	4/1/2004	Present	No
Batson	30.251	-94.607	5	COOP	7/1/1992	12/1/1998	No
Beaumont # 2	30.126	-94.090	0	COOP	1/1/1985	6/28/2006	No
Beaumont City	30.097	-94.100	6	COOP	11/1/1901	Present	No
Beaumont Research Ctr.	30.069	-94.293	8	COOP	9/1/1946	Present	No
Cleveland	30.364	-95.084	60	COOP	6/1/1954	Present	No
Cleveland 1 WSW	30.333	-95.100	55	COOP	6/1/1976	9/21/1985	No
Coldspring 5 SSW	30.533	-95.150	108	COOP	6/1/1954	3/1/2002	No
Evadale	30.333	-94.083	10	COOP	8/26/1944	6/30/2006	No
Evadale 1 W	30.356	-94.093	2	COOP	9/1/1984	7/1/2006	No
Goodrich 3 S	30.571	-94.950	24	COOP	1/1/1970	Present	No
Horger	31.000	-94.167	34	COOP	8/27/1944	1/1/1983	No
Hyatt	30.567	-94.400	34	COOP	4/1/1935	11/30/1953	No
Jasper	30.915	-94.010	88	COOP	9/20/1878	Present	No
Jasper 2 E	30.917	-93.967	67	COOP	12/1/1948	5/31/1953	No
Kirbyville	30.617	-93.917	61	COOP	1/1/1929	3/1/1999	No
Kountze	30.400	-94.333	27	COOP	12/1/1979	12/31/1982	No

Name	Lat.	Lon.	Elev. (m)	Network	Start	End	In Park?
Kountze	30.375	-94.299	19	COOP	7/1/1947	Present	No
Kountze 3 NE	30.398	-94.263	8	COOP	6/1/1988	7/1/2006	No
Lakeview	30.223	-94.114	3	COOP	2/1/2004	11/1/2004	No
Liberty	30.059	-94.795	11	COOP	10/1/1903	Present	No
Liberty #2	30.050	-94.817	1	COOP	7/1/1985	Present	No
Liberty 6 NE	30.133	-94.733	17	COOP	3/30/1978	10/1/1978	No
Livingston 2 NNE	30.739	-94.926	54	COOP	3/1/1937	Present	No
Lumberton	30.250	-94.179	12	COOP	11/1/1995	Present	No
Moscow	30.917	-94.833	76	COOP	6/4/1940	4/30/1975	No
Port Arthur SE Tx. Regl. Arpt.	29.951	-94.021	5	COOP	3/1/1944	Present	No
Romayor 1 WSW	30.433	-94.850	18	COOP	9/1/1969	Present	No
Sam Rayburn Dam	31.062	-94.101	58	COOP	5/1/1967	Present	No
Shepherd	30.483	-95.000	55	COOP	4/18/1940	2/15/1965	No
Silsbee 4 N	30.370	-94.202	55	COOP	11/1/1995	Present	No
Sour Lake 5 SE	30.100	-94.333	0	COOP	8/1/1948	Present	No
Town Bluff Dam	30.800	-94.183	65	COOP	7/1/1953	Present	No
Warren 2 S	30.583	-94.400	34	COOP	5/1/1935	6/30/1992	No
Wildwood	30.516	-94.438	61	COOP	2/1/1992	Present	No
Woodville	30.768	-94.412	86	COOP	9/1/1988	Present	No
Woodville	30.783	-94.433	70	COOP	4/1/1917	2/28/1919	No
CW4340 Silsbee	30.383	-94.167	26	CWOP	M	Present	No
KD5HQQ Rye	30.488	-94.777	37	CWOP	M	Present	No
Beaumont	30.160	-94.180	16	GPS-MET	M	Present	No
Coldsprings	30.311	-95.087	44	RAWS	11/1/2001	Present	No
Kirbyville	30.433	-93.883	91	RAWS	1/1/2001	Present	No
Woodville	30.750	-94.400	116	RAWS	12/1/2000	Present	No
Jasper Co. Bell Field Arpt.	30.886	-94.035	65	SAO	12/1/1999	Present	No
Port Arthur SE Tx. Regl. Arpt.	29.951	-94.021	5	SAO	3/1/1944	Present	No
Beaumont	30.083	-94.217	10	WBAN	2/1/1929	12/31/1978	No
Gulf Islands National Seashore – GUIS							
Pensacola Beach	30.333	-87.133	3	COOP	8/1/1957	12/31/1964	Yes
Fort Pickens	30.318	-87.255	7	POMS	8/1/2004	9/30/2005	Yes
Naval Live Oaks	30.366	-87.138	5	RAWS	2/1/2003	5/31/2005	Yes
Santa Rosa Gulf Breeze	30.317	-87.250	2	SAO	7/1/1935	Present	Yes
Santa Rosa Site A-11	30.400	-86.717	4	WBAN	9/1/1960	10/31/1964	Yes
Pensacola Beach	30.330	-87.160	1	WX4U	M	Present	Yes
Biloxi	30.393	-89.001	3	COOP	5/1/1893	Present	No
Biloxi 2	30.400	-88.867	3	COOP	11/1/1966	8/31/1969	No
Biloxi 9 WNW	30.438	-89.028	6	COOP	4/1/1970	Present	No
Biloxi Display	30.400	-88.883	8	COOP	1/1/1948	Present	No
Cantonment	30.600	-87.317	46	COOP	1/1/1949	3/31/1952	No
Chandeleur Lighthouse	30.050	-88.867	0	COOP	9/1/1937	8/31/1949	No
Coden	30.388	-88.228	4	COOP	10/1/1956	Present	No
Cottage Hill	30.450	-87.333	40	COOP	11/1/1921	1/31/1942	No

Name	Lat.	Lon.	Elev. (m)	Network	Start	End	In Park?
Dauphin I. Bridge	30.283	-88.133	2	COOP	5/1/1968	12/31/1979	No
Dauphin Island #2	30.250	-88.083	2	COOP	7/1/1961	Present	No
Fort Walton Beach	30.417	-86.633	7	COOP	8/1/1957	Present	No
Fort Walton Beach	30.433	-86.600	6	COOP	M	10/31/1966	No
Garniers (Near)	30.467	-86.600	5	COOP	10/1/1912	4/30/1938	No
Gulf Shores P.O.	30.283	-87.683	3	COOP	8/1/1948	1/31/1975	No
Gulfport	30.367	-89.100	0	COOP	M	Present	No
Gulfport - Biloxi Arpt.	30.412	-89.081	13	COOP	9/25/2000	Present	No
Gulfport 3 NW	30.454	-89.125	8	COOP	8/1/1997	Present	No
Gulfport A.	30.417	-89.067	8	COOP	5/1/1935	6/13/1956	No
Gulfport Naval Ctr.	30.377	-89.123	11	COOP	6/30/1956	Present	No
Milton	30.617	-87.033	0	COOP	3/1/1956	Present	No
Moss Point	30.400	-88.500	6	COOP	1/1/1887	5/31/1899	No
Niceville	30.531	-86.492	18	COOP	2/1/1927	Present	No
Ocean Springs	30.411	-88.788	3	COOP	1/1/1994	Present	No
Pascagoula 3 NE	30.396	-88.478	4	COOP	2/1/1909	Present	No
Pascagoula Churn	30.350	-88.567	9	COOP	11/21/1958	Present	No
Pascagoula Lott Intl. Arpt.	30.464	-88.532	5	COOP	7/1/1961	Present	No
Pascagoula Sp. Yd.	30.350	-88.567	3	COOP	10/1/1947	11/30/1960	No
Pecan	30.433	-88.433	0	COOP	7/1/1901	6/30/1908	No
Pensacola	30.417	-87.217	16	COOP	1/1/1893	10/10/1963	No
Pensacola Regl. Arpt.	30.478	-87.187	34	COOP	4/1/1937	Present	No
Valparaiso Eglin AFB	30.483	-86.517	18	COOP	9/1/1938	Present	No
Vancleave	30.486	-88.655	3	COOP	5/24/1940	8/29/2005	No
CW1141 Pensacola	30.406	-87.391	6	CWOP	M	Present	No
CW1231 Lillian	30.376	-87.477	11	CWOP	M	Present	No
CW1258 Seminole	30.522	-87.465	29	CWOP	M	Present	No
CW1640 Niceville	30.477	-86.415	7	CWOP	M	Present	No
CW2010 Navarre	30.414	-86.874	8	CWOP	M	Present	No
CW2227 Gulf Breeze	30.379	-87.065	15	CWOP	M	Present	No
CW3964 Cantonment	30.542	-87.299	38	CWOP	M	Present	No
CW3968 Altoona	30.453	-86.397	16	CWOP	M	Present	No
CW3969 Altoona	30.453	-86.397	16	CWOP	M	Present	No
CW4163 Gulf Breeze	30.400	-86.955	7	CWOP	M	Present	No
CW4807 Shalimar	30.441	-86.567	6	CWOP	M	Present	No
KD4YJJ-2 Pensacola	30.452	-87.217	26	CWOP	M	Present	No
KF4YEP-3 Pensacola	30.401	-87.679	6	CWOP	M	Present	No
KF4YEP-7 Pensacola	30.426	-87.284	27	CWOP	M	Present	No
KG4SEY Niceville	30.489	-86.426	17	CWOP	M	Present	No
KI4JFS Niceville	30.477	-86.415	3	CWOP	M	Present	No
N9OSQ-7 Pensacola	30.473	-87.235	32	CWOP	M	Present	No
W4RL-1 Pensacola	30.514	-87.176	23	CWOP	M	Present	No
W8JE Pass Christian	30.367	-89.220	5	CWOP	M	Present	No
WB4QEV-2 Mobile	30.244	-88.077	10	CWOP	M	Present	No
WB4QEV-3 Grand Bay	30.443	-88.284	27	CWOP	M	Present	No
Grand Bay	30.429	-88.429	5	RAWS	2/1/2003	5/31/2005	No

Name	Lat.	Lon.	Elev. (m)	Network	Start	End	In Park?
Gulfport Arpt. (FRWS5)	30.412	-89.081	9	RAWS	9/1/2005	Present	No
Sandhill Crane	30.453	-88.662	8	RAWS	12/1/2002	Present	No
Barin Field NAAS	30.400	-87.600	22	SAO	2/1/1945	9/30/1958	No
Destin Fort Walton Beach Arpt.	30.400	-86.472	7	SAO	11/6/1996	Present	No
Duke Field AAFB	30.650	-86.533	58	SAO	9/1/1949	Present	No
Gulfport - Biloxi Arpt.	30.412	-89.081	13	SAO	9/25/2000	Present	No
Gulfport LAS	30.367	-89.083	1	SAO	9/1/1943	Present	No
Keesler AFB	30.417	-88.917	8	SAO	5/1/1942	Present	No
Pascagoula Lott Intl. Arpt.	30.464	-88.532	5	SAO	7/1/1961	Present	No
Pascagoula Stn.	30.367	-88.567	8	SAO	M	Present	No
Pensacola Chevalier Fld. NAS	30.350	-87.267	21	SAO	1/1/1921	5/31/1955	No
Pensacola Corry Fld. NAAS	30.400	-87.283	11	SAO	2/1/1945	5/31/1958	No
Pensacola Ellyson Fld. NAAS	30.533	-87.200	40	SAO	1/1/1952	12/31/1973	No
Pensacola Forest Sherman NAS	30.350	-87.317	10	SAO	1/1/1949	Present	No
Pensacola Regl. Arpt.	30.478	-87.187	34	SAO	4/1/1937	Present	No
Pensacola Saufley NAS	30.483	-87.350	28	SAO	11/1/1948	9/30/1976	No
Valparaiso Eglin AFB	30.483	-86.517	18	SAO	9/1/1938	Present	No
Valparaiso Hurlburt	30.417	-86.683	12	SAO	7/1/1955	Present	No
TNC Fort Bayou	30.470	-88.740	13	SCAN	M	Present	No
Biloxi	30.400	-88.917	7	WBAN	2/1/1938	5/31/1948	No
Eglin Aux. F6	30.617	-86.733	42	WBAN	9/1/1949	10/31/1949	No
Eglin Range 70 Mobile	30.583	-86.650	67	WBAN	9/1/1960	10/31/1964	No
Eglin Range 75	30.550	-86.750	59	WBAN	3/1/1961	3/31/1965	No
Eglin Site A-15 Mobile	30.483	-86.800	4	WBAN	9/1/1960	9/30/1964	No
Gulfport AAF	30.400	-89.067	13	WBAN	9/1/1943	12/31/1945	No
Pensacola Bronson Field NAAS	30.383	-87.417	12	WBAN	3/1/1945	12/31/1945	No
Pierce Field AAFB	30.517	-86.433	48	WBAN	9/1/1949	11/30/1949	No
Pierce Field AAFB	30.583	-86.450	48	WBAN	1/1/1953	12/31/1957	No
Valparaiso	30.433	-86.933	12	WBAN	2/1/1967	Present	No
Eglin AFB Rng. 52	30.567	-86.317	55	WBAN	M	Present	No
Grand Bay	30.470	-88.340	21	WX4U	M	Present	No
Santa Rosa Sound Navarre	30.401	-86.864	4	WX4U	M	Present	No

Jean Lafitte National Historical Park and Preserve – JELA

Name	Lat.	Lon.	Elev. (m)	Network	Start	End	In Park?
Marrero 9 SSW	29.785	-90.116	1	COOP	2/1/1988	Present	Yes
Abbeville	29.969	-92.117	3	COOP	2/1/1891	Present	No
Andrew	30.083	-92.250	6	COOP	2/21/1943	1/1/1970	No
Basile 2 W	30.483	-92.633	1	COOP	1/1/1943	6/7/2005	No
Belle Chasse	29.883	-90.000	0	COOP	7/1/1946	1/31/1949	No
Breaux Bridge 4 S	30.223	-91.903	8	COOP	11/1/1995	12/1/2002	No
Butte La Rose	30.282	-91.691	2	COOP	4/1/1973	Present	No
Cades	30.100	-91.900	0	COOP	6/1/1910	12/31/1919	No

Name	Lat.	Lon.	Elev. (m)	Network	Start	End	In Park?
Carencro	30.316	-92.048	15	COOP	3/1/1986	Present	No
Chalmette	29.966	-89.976	0	COOP	7/1/1991	8/29/2005	No
Convent 2 S	29.995	-90.816	8	COOP	9/1/1996	Present	No
Crowley 2 NE	30.241	-92.348	8	COOP	6/1/1906	Present	No
Dalcour	29.817	-90.000	24	COOP	8/1/1929	11/30/1930	No
Delta Farms	29.600	-90.350	0	COOP	6/1/1911	8/31/1947	No
Easton	30.750	-92.417	27	COOP	5/1/1920	3/31/1921	No
Eunice	30.492	-92.430	15	COOP	5/14/1940	Present	No
Gheens	29.700	-90.467	3	COOP	4/1/1947	1/31/1951	No
Grand Coteau	30.418	-92.041	17	COOP	1/1/1893	Present	No
Gretna	29.917	-90.062	2	COOP	9/1/1983	Present	No
Henderson 2 W	30.317	-91.817	6	COOP	3/1/1962	1/31/1967	No
Houma	29.586	-90.730	5	COOP	1/1/1893	Present	No
Houma 2	29.583	-90.733	3	COOP	7/1/1947	9/10/1954	No
Lacombe	30.300	-89.883	6	COOP	10/28/1983	5/22/1987	No
Lacombe 2 SSW	30.283	-89.950	0	COOP	4/1/1957	11/30/1957	No
Lafayette	30.219	-92.065	8	COOP	3/1/1952	Present	No
Lafayette 2 S	30.233	-92.000	0	COOP	7/1/1947	12/8/1961	No
Lafayette Regl. Arpt.	30.205	-91.988	12	COOP	1/1/1893	Present	No
Louisiana Nature Ctr.	30.031	-89.964	-2	COOP	1/1/1981	8/29/2005	No
Lutcher	30.039	-90.694	6	COOP	4/1/1985	Present	No
Mamou 4 S	30.567	-92.433	18	COOP	7/1/1970	7/1/1982	No
Metairie	29.990	-90.143	0	COOP	12/1/1949	8/28/2005	No
Napoleonville	29.934	-91.016	8	COOP	7/21/1895	Present	No
Naval Ammunition Dept.	29.883	-89.983	0	COOP	4/16/1943	5/31/1960	No
New Orleans Algiers	29.952	-90.050	1	COOP	7/1/1946	Present	No
New Orleans Alvin Callender Fi.	29.817	-90.017	2	COOP	4/1/1947	Present	No
New Orleans Audubon	29.917	-90.130	6	COOP	1/1/1893	Present	No
New Orleans Carrltn.	29.935	-90.136	0	COOP	5/1/1893	6/1/2005	No
New Orleans D P S 3	29.983	-90.067	3	COOP	7/1/1946	12/31/1990	No
New Orleans D P S 5	29.983	-90.017	3	COOP	7/1/1946	12/31/1990	No
New Orleans Eastover	30.049	-89.952	-2	COOP	7/1/1961	5/1/2002	No
New Orleans Intl. Arpt.	29.993	-90.251	1	COOP	5/1/1946	Present	No
New Orleans Jefferson	29.933	-90.100	3	COOP	7/1/1946	6/30/1978	No
New Orleans Lakefront Arpt.	30.049	-90.029	3	COOP	3/1/1932	Present	No
New Orleans Park	29.933	-90.117	9	COOP	7/1/1932	4/30/1975	No
New Orleans Pines Vil.	30.017	-90.017	-1	COOP	7/1/1954	6/30/1961	No
New Orleans S&WB	29.950	-90.050	2	COOP	M	12/31/1990	No
New Orleans Water Plant	29.950	-90.133	6	COOP	7/1/1946	12/31/1990	No
New Orleans WSFO City	29.950	-90.083	1	COOP	6/1/1888	4/24/1979	No
Paradis 7 S	29.789	-90.428	2	COOP	7/1/1911	Present	No
Pontchartrain Causeway	30.250	-90.117	9	COOP	11/1/1956	4/1/1966	No
Pontchartrain Grove	30.050	-89.617	0	COOP	6/1/1917	10/31/1918	No
Prevost Island	30.200	-89.733	3	COOP	6/1/1899	7/31/1902	No
Rayne 6 N	30.333	-92.267	9	COOP	M	4/30/1968	No

Name	Lat.	Lon.	Elev. (m)	Network	Start	End	In Park?
Rigolets	30.183	-89.717	1	COOP	7/22/1957	10/31/1964	No
Schriever	29.733	-90.817	6	COOP	1/1/1893	10/22/1974	No
Slidell	30.265	-89.770	3	COOP	1/1/1956	Present	No
Southern Univ. Farm	29.950	-90.150	3	COOP	11/1/1894	9/30/1914	No
St. Martinville 3 SW	30.086	-91.869	9	COOP	3/1/1985	Present	No
St. Bernard	29.872	-89.830	2	COOP	2/1/1966	8/29/2005	No
Terrytown 3 S	29.853	-90.028	3	COOP	8/1/1997	Present	No
Thibodaux # 2	29.800	-90.817	6	COOP	1/1/1983	Present	No
Thibodaux # 2	29.800	-90.817	6	COOP	1/1/1893	9/1/1981	No
Thibodaux 3 ESE	29.776	-90.780	5	COOP	9/1/1981	Present	No
Ville Platte	30.694	-92.282	21	COOP	4/1/1926	Present	No
Violet	29.917	-89.900	3	COOP	3/1/1955	1/1/1969	No
Lafayette 13 SE	30.092	-91.873	11	CRN	1/10/2003	Present	No
AD5DP Slidell	30.254	-89.786	7	CWOP	M	Present	No
CW1536 Belle Chasse	29.827	-90.008	2	CWOP	M	Present	No
CW1548 Gretna	29.860	-90.030	2	CWOP	M	Present	No
CW1615 Lafayette	30.212	-92.060	13	CWOP	M	Present	No
CW2242 Schriever	29.667	-90.818	3	CWOP	M	Present	No
CW2378 New Orleans	29.969	-90.218	2	CWOP	M	Present	No
CW2867 Lafayette	30.142	-92.057	12	CWOP	M	Present	No
CW3916 Belle Chasse	29.834	-90.002	1	CWOP	M	Present	No
CW4185 New Orleans	29.950	-90.199	3	CWOP	M	Present	No
CW5524 Terrytown	29.912	-90.033	-2	CWOP	M	Present	No
CW5600 Paulina	30.039	-90.715	6	CWOP	M	Present	No
CW5836 Deer Range	29.596	-89.906	2	CWOP	M	Present	No
N8OVD St. Martinsville	30.051	-91.818	10	CWOP	M	Present	No
W5MLE Carencro	30.332	-92.052	14	CWOP	M	Present	No
English Turn	29.880	-89.940	7	GPS-MET	M	Present	No
Lafayette	30.220	-92.050	20	GPS-MET	M	Present	No
Big Branch NWR	30.317	-89.933	3	RAWS	12/1/2002	Present	No
New Orleans Airport (FRWS-9)	29.990	-90.262	1	RAWS	9/1/2005	Present	No
Plaquemines Parrish	29.854	-89.982	2	RAWS	9/1/2005	Present	No
Lafayette Regl. Arpt.	30.205	-91.988	12	SAO	1/1/1893	Present	No
Lake Palourd Base Heliport	29.693	-91.099	2	SAO	3/22/2005	Present	No
New Iberia Acadiana Regl. Arpt.	30.038	-91.884	7	SAO	12/15/1970	Present	No
New Iberia NAAS	30.033	-91.883	8	SAO	1/1/1961	10/31/1964	No
New Orleans AAB Lakefront	30.033	-90.033	3	SAO	9/1/1942	2/28/1944	No
New Orleans Alvin Callender Fi.	29.817	-90.017	2	SAO	4/1/1947	Present	No
New Orleans Intl. Arpt.	29.993	-90.251	1	SAO	5/1/1946	Present	No
New Orleans Lakefront Arpt.	30.049	-90.029	3	SAO	3/1/1932	Present	No
New Orleans WSFO City	29.950	-90.083	1	SAO	6/1/1888	4/24/1979	No
Slidell	30.265	-89.770	3	SAO	1/1/1956	Present	No
Houma NAS	29.567	-90.667	12	WBAN	6/1/1943	7/31/1945	No

Name	Lat.	Lon.	Elev. (m)	Network	Start	End	In Park?
New Orleans NAS	30.033	-90.083	4	WBAN	11/1/1942	11/30/1957	No
Vicksburg National Military Park – VICK							
Vicksburg Military P.	32.357	-90.844	78	COOP	7/1/1967	2/1/2004	Yes
Warren	32.356	-90.844	76	RAWS	1/1/2004	Present	Yes
Rose Hill	32.367	-90.833	0	COOP	5/1/1933	4/30/1936	No
Vicksburg	32.314	-90.905	14	COOP	1/1/1892	4/25/2002	No
Vicksburg	32.350	-90.883	90	COOP	8/1/1872	6/30/1967	No
Vicksburg City	32.385	-90.875	24	COOP	4/1/1969	Present	No
Vicksburg Waterways	32.298	-90.866	55	COOP	M	11/30/2004	No
Vicksburg Old	32.400	-90.783	37	COOP	7/1/1935	9/30/1950	No
Mound	32.333	-91.017	27	COOP	5/1/1914	9/30/1915	No
Bovina	32.350	-90.700	49	COOP	12/1/1966	Present	No
Edwards	32.317	-90.617	76	COOP	4/1/1882	11/30/1920	No
Valley Park	32.633	-90.867	0	COOP	6/1/1940	8/31/1947	No
Tallulah	32.399	-91.184	26	COOP	8/13/1907	Present	No
Satartia 8 SW	32.586	-90.626	43	COOP	8/1/2002	Present	No
Vicksburg	32.233	-90.933	31	COOP	6/1/1950	Present	No
Tallulah Vicksburg Regl. Arpt.	32.350	-91.028	26	COOP	2/29/1996	Present	No
Vicksburg	32.330	-90.920	36	GPS-MET	M	Present	No
Vicksburg	32.233	-90.933	31	SAO	6/1/1950	Present	No
Tallulah Vicksburg Regl Arpt.	32.350	-91.028	26	SAO	2/29/1996	Present	No

Several other automated stations are located within 30 km of the various BITH units. The CASTNet station "Alabama-Coushatta" has been active since 2004 (Table 4.4) and is located 4 km southwest of the Turkey Creek unit (Figure 4.2). Three RAWS stations are located within 30 km of BITH units. One of these (Kirbyville) is located 19 km east of the easternmost unit of BITH. The other two RAWS stations ("Coldsprings" and "Woodville") are located north and west of BITH units. "Coldsprings" is located 30 km west of the Big Sandy Creek unit, while "Woodville" is about 15 km north of the Turkey Creek unit and 15 km west of the Beech Creek unit. Two SAO stations have been identified within 30 km of BITH. These include "Jasper Co. Bell Field Arpt.," located 15 km northeast of the Upper Neches River Corridor unit, and "Port Arthur SE Tx.," located 25 km southeast of the Beaumont unit.

Out of the 36 COOP stations identified within 30 km of the outer boundary of BITH, 18 are currently active (Table 4.4). The closest active COOP station is "Town Bluff Dam," located less than 1 km north of the Upper Neches River Corridor unit of BITH. This station has been active since 1953. The longest record among these active COOP stations, going back to 1878, is found at "Jasper." This station is 19 km northeast of the Upper Neches River Corridor unit of BITH (Figure 4.2).Unfortunately, a major data gap occurred at this station from 1905 to 1948. In addition to this, "Jasper" has not measured temperatures since July 1973. "Liberty" is located 27 km southwest of the Loblolly unit of BITH and has a data record going back to 1903. The data record at "Liberty" is very complete. A third long-term record of note is found at the COOP station "Livingston 2 NNE," located 21 km northwest of the Big Sandy Creek unit. The data

Figure 4.2. Station locations for the GULN park units in east Texas and the Gulf Coast states.

record at this station goes back to 1937 and, like "Liberty," is very complete. Several other COOP stations within 30 km of BITH have data records that are over 50 years in length.

Six stations were identified within GUIS (Table 4.4). All of these stations are located on the Florida units of GUIS (Figure 4.2). The only active stations we identified are a SAO station (Santa Rosa Gulf Breeze) and a WX4U station (Pensacola Beach). The SAO station has been active since 1935, providing a long-term climate record for the Florida units of GUIS.

Outside of GUIS, we identified 32 COOP stations within 30 km of the park unit boundaries. Eighteen of these stations are currently active (Table 4.4). The active COOP station with the longest data record is "Biloxi," which is 10 km north of the Mississippi units of GUIS (Figure 4.2). This station has several data gaps during the 1980s and early 1990s. The largest of these gaps include a gap in temperature observations from December 1988 to August 1991, and a gap in precipitation observations from December 1988 to March 1990. Another long-term record available to the Mississippi units of GUIS is found at the COOP station "Pascagoula 3 NE." This station is 19 km north of the Mississippi units and has been operating since 1909. This station has had a very complete data record over the past 30 years, with only occasional data gaps before then. The Florida units of GUIS also have some useful long-term climate records available to them. The longest of these is found at the COOP station "Niceville," which is 14 km north of the Florida units and has been operating since 1927. A gap in temperature observations occurred from April 1990 to April 1993; otherwise, the station's record is very complete. Other long-term records are found at the COOP stations "Pensacola Regl. Arpt." and "Valparaiso Eglin AFB," located 12 km and 8 km, respectively, north of the Florida units. The data records at both stations are very complete. Several other COOP stations within 30 km of GUIS have data records that are over 50 years in length.

Numerous sources of near-real-time weather data are available for GUIS. Of the three RAWS stations we identified within 30 km of GUIS, two are still active (Table 4.4). "Gulfport Arpt. (FRWS5)" is 23 km north of the Mississippi units (Figure 4.2). "Sandhill Crane" is northwest of Pascagoula, Mississippi, about 12 km north of the Mississippi units. An active SCAN station (TNC Fort Bayou) is located 7 km north of GUIS units in Mississippi and provides near-real-time weather data. At least 11 active SAO sites also provide near-real-time data within 30 km of GUIS. Five of these stations are within 30 km of the Mississippi units, while the remaining six stations are within 30 km of the Florida units. In addition to these stations, we have identified two WX4U stations and 21 CWOP stations that provide near-real-time data within 30 km of GUIS units.

Jean Lafitte National Historical Park and Preserve (JELA) has one weather/climate station inside its park unit boundaries (Table 4.4). This is a COOP station (Marrero 9 SSW), located in the Beretaria Preserve. This station has been active since 1988. No stations provide near-real-time weather data within JELA.

Fortunately, there are several weather networks that provide near-real-time data within 30 km of JELA units. The CRN station "Lafayette 13 SE" is 18 km southeast of the Acadian Cultural Center in Lafayette, Louisiana (Figure 4.2). The three RAWS stations we have identified for JELA (Table 4.4) are located within 30 km of New Orleans. "Big Branch NWR" is 27 km north of the city, across Lake Pontchartrain. The other two RAWS stations, "New Orleans Airport (FRWS-9)" and "Plaquemines Parrish," are south of New Orleans. Several SAO stations are located within 30 km of JELA units. These stations are associated primarily with airports around Lafayette and New Orleans.

We identified 29 COOP stations, of which 12 are active currently, within 30 km of the park unit boundaries (Table 4.4). The active COOP station with the longest data record is "Abbeville," which is 30 km southwest of the Acadian Cultural Center (Figure 4.2). This station measures only precipitation. The data record at "Abbeville" has been most complete after 1970, with occasional data gaps before that time. Three other COOP stations of note have data records going back to the 1890s, with each of these records being very complete. "Grand Coteau" and "Lafayette Regl. Arpt." are 23 km north and 1 km east, respectively, of the Acadian Cultural Center in Lafayette, Louisiana. "Houma" is located 25 km southeast of the Wetlands Acadian Cultural Center. Another long-term record from the COOP station "Crowley 2 NE" is available 29 km south of the Prairie Acadian Cultural Center in Eunice, Louisiana. This station has a data record going back to 1906 but this record has a significant gap in temperature observations from January 1955 to March 1968. Several other COOP stations within 30 km of JELA have data records that are over 50 years in length.

We have identified two weather/climate stations within VICK (Table 4.4). The COOP station we identified (Vicksburg Military P.) is no longer active (1967-2004), while the RAWS station we identified (Warren) is active and provides near-real-time weather data for VICK.

We have identified six COOP stations within 30 km of VICK (Table 4.4). The COOP station "Tallulah," 29 km west of VICK, provides the longest period of record of the active COOP stations in the area, having operated since 1907. A long-term COOP station "Vicksburg" had operated from 1892 until 2002. A separate COOP station, also named "Vicksburg," is currently active and its period of record extends back to 1950.

We have identified at least two sources of near-real-time weather data within 30 km of VICK (Table 4.4). The SAO station "Vicksburg" is located 9 km southwest of VICK (Figure 4.2) and has been active since 1950, while the SAO station "Tallulah Vicksburg Regl. Arpt." is 13 km west of VICK and has been active since 1996.

4.2.3. Natchez Trace Parkway
We have identified three weather/climate stations inside the boundaries of NATR (Table 4.5). Two of these are historical COOP stations, while the third station is an active RAWS station. The COOP station "Washington" was located about 10 km east of Natchez, Mississippi, while the COOP station "Bishop" was located in northwestern Alabama, only a couple kilometers east of the Alabama/Mississippi border. The RAWS station identified along NATR is located about 35 km southwest of Tupelo, Mississippi, at the junction of NATR with Highway 41. This station has been active since 1997.

Just over 40 percent of the 158 COOP stations identified within 30 km of NATR are active currently (Table 4.5). The closest active COOP station to NATR is "Tupelo 2," located less than 1 km from the parkway in northeastern Mississippi. We identified numerous active COOP stations with data records greater than 50 years in length. Several of these stations have data records going back to the 1890s. Due to the larger number of stations identified for NATR, we will limit our discussion to those stations having data records starting in the 1890s.

Table 4.5. Weather/climate stations for NATR. Stations inside NATR and within 30 km of NATR boundary are included. Missing entries are indicated by "M".

Natchez Trace Parkway – NATR							
Name	Lat.	Lon.	Elev. (m)	Network	Start	End	In Park?
Bishop	34.650	-88.117	143	COOP	1/1/1937	3/31/1962	Yes
Washington	31.583	-91.283	85	COOP	1/1/1890	8/31/1945	Yes
Highway 41	34.090	-88.865	98	RAWS	5/1/1997	Present	Yes
Ackerman	33.312	-89.163	171	COOP	2/1/1940	Present	No
Alcorn A & M College	31.883	-91.150	79	COOP	10/1/1952	7/1/1972	No
Ashwood	35.583	-87.133	223	COOP	5/1/1890	3/31/1977	No
Baldwyn	34.483	-88.639	110	COOP	2/1/1940	Present	No
Barton	34.717	-87.867	140	COOP	1/1/1949	5/31/1953	No
Belgreen	34.467	-87.867	247	COOP	3/1/1935	3/31/1962	No
Bellefontaine 2 NNW	33.667	-89.333	122	COOP	6/1/1906	4/30/1951	No
Belmont 2 SSE	34.477	-88.199	187	COOP	7/1/1948	Present	No
Booneville	34.669	-88.570	149	COOP	7/3/1892	Present	No
Bovina	32.350	-90.700	49	COOP	12/1/1966	Present	No
Brentwood	35.990	-86.779	215	COOP	11/1/1995	Present	No
Briers	31.383	-91.383	18	COOP	12/1/1892	8/31/1899	No
Burnsville Substn.	34.833	-88.317	143	COOP	7/1/1948	3/31/1962	No
Cairo	34.700	-88.350	162	COOP	4/1/1959	3/31/1962	No
Calhoun City	33.859	-89.316	78	COOP	1/1/1915	Present	No
Canton 4 N	32.671	-90.036	76	COOP	7/1/1892	Present	No
Carthage	32.751	-89.539	113	COOP	8/1/1955	Present	No
Carthage 2 S	32.707	-89.526	96	COOP	10/1/1962	Present	No
Center	32.933	-89.450	0	COOP	1/1/1948	8/31/1948	No
Centerville	35.783	-87.467	192	COOP	8/1/1948	10/31/1954	No
Centerville 2	35.767	-87.467	137	COOP	2/1/1976	4/30/1985	No
Centerville 4 NE	35.832	-87.422	226	COOP	1/31/2000	Present	No
Centerville Water Plant	35.755	-87.426	201	COOP	1/1/1949	7/26/2006	No
Charlotte	36.172	-87.181	212	COOP	6/5/2006	Present	No
Clayton	31.724	-91.541	22	COOP	4/17/1998	Present	No
Clifton Junction	35.317	-87.917	143	COOP	1/1/1949	3/31/1962	No
Clinton Exp. Stn.	32.300	-90.317	98	COOP	3/1/1944	12/31/1971	No
Colbert Steam Plant	34.750	-87.850	143	COOP	11/1/1951	12/9/1980	No
Collinwood	35.183	-87.733	290	COOP	2/1/1949	3/31/1962	No
Columbia 2 W	35.617	-87.083	195	COOP	2/1/1950	1/31/1952	No
Columbia 3 WNW	35.639	-87.087	198	COOP	6/2/1948	Present	No
Columbia Substn.	35.667	-87.033	189	COOP	1/1/1949	3/31/1962	No
Columbia Wkrm.	35.617	-87.033	204	COOP	1/1/1949	1/1/1972	No
Crystal Springs 4 N	32.033	-90.317	113	COOP	10/1/1954	10/31/1984	No

Natchez Trace Parkway – NATR

Name	Lat.	Lon.	Elev. (m)	Network	Start	End	In Park?
Dancy	33.667	-89.050	88	COOP	6/29/1942	12/31/1989	No
Durant	33.083	-89.850	82	COOP	10/1/1930	6/30/1947	No
Eastport	34.917	-88.183	137	COOP	10/1/1943	12/31/1948	No
Edinburg	32.799	-89.337	107	COOP	12/1/1907	Present	No
Edwards	32.317	-90.617	76	COOP	4/1/1882	11/30/1920	No
Ellistown	34.467	-88.833	112	COOP	10/1/1980	9/30/1990	No
Ethel	33.117	-89.472	130	COOP	6/1/1980	Present	No
Ethridge	35.317	-87.300	299	COOP	9/1/1948	3/31/1962	No
Eupora 2 E	33.563	-89.236	134	COOP	3/1/1927	Present	No
Fairview Bowie Nat. Ctr.	35.986	-87.136	262	COOP	8/1/2001	Present	No
Fayette	31.683	-91.067	85	COOP	12/1/1892	Present	No
Ferriday	31.633	-91.567	0	COOP	4/1/1907	3/31/1913	No
Flora	32.533	-90.317	67	COOP	1/1/1948	5/31/1950	No
Florence	34.800	-87.683	177	COOP	1/1/1893	4/30/1977	No
Florence At Lock	34.783	-87.667	137	COOP	12/25/1890	11/30/1959	No
Forest Hills Dyer Obsv.	36.056	-86.807	344	COOP	2/9/2001	Present	No
Franklin 2	35.921	-86.865	189	COOP	5/1/1975	2/25/2002	No
Franklin 3 NE	35.950	-86.817	229	COOP	1/2/1949	3/31/1962	No
Franklin 5 NE	35.967	-86.800	229	COOP	10/15/1953	3/31/1962	No
Franklin Sewage Plant	35.948	-86.870	200	COOP	8/1/1891	Present	No
Fulton 3 W	34.261	-88.457	107	COOP	12/1/1894	Present	No
Goshen Springs 3 NW	32.505	-89.928	98	COOP	9/1/1946	Present	No
Guntown 3 NW	34.484	-88.704	131	COOP	11/1/1980	Present	No
Hohenwald	35.557	-87.541	299	COOP	1/1/1893	Present	No
Houston	33.928	-89.008	83	COOP	1/1/1942	Present	No
Iron City	35.017	-87.583	186	COOP	1/1/1949	3/31/1962	No
Iuka 5 S	34.825	-88.191	143	COOP	4/1/1959	Present	No
Jackson 1 SSE	32.282	-90.179	71	COOP	7/1/1948	11/12/2002	No
Jackson 4 NW	32.333	-90.233	98	COOP	1/1/1909	1/1/1972	No
Jackson Hawkins Field	32.337	-90.221	104	COOP	9/1/1942	Present	No
Jackson Intl. Arpt.	32.321	-90.078	101	COOP	7/1/1963	Present	No
Jackson State	32.296	-90.209	99	COOP	10/1/2002	Present	No
Kingston Springs	36.104	-87.115	158	COOP	2/7/1941	Present	No
Kosciusko	33.058	-89.580	125	COOP	1/1/1893	Present	No
Kosciusko 13 SE	32.984	-89.390	128	COOP	6/1/1980	Present	No
Kosciusko 2 SSE	33.033	-89.578	114	COOP	5/1/1980	4/24/2002	No
L Argent	31.750	-91.400	21	COOP	5/1/1899	6/30/1901	No
Lawrenceburg	35.233	-87.317	256	COOP	1/1/1949	3/31/1962	No
Lawrenceburg Filt. Plant	35.264	-87.351	265	COOP	10/1/1954	Present	No
Little Rock 5 SSE	33.463	-88.980	113	COOP	3/5/1981	Present	No
Loretto	35.083	-87.433	256	COOP	12/1/1895	3/31/1962	No
Lorman	31.817	-91.050	70	COOP	1/1/1951	10/1/1969	No

Natchez Trace Parkway – NATR

Name	Lat.	Lon.	Elev. (m)	Network	Start	End	In Park?
Madison Stn. 2 SSW	32.433	-90.133	104	COOP	6/1/1948	10/31/1951	No
McGlamery	35.150	-87.750	290	COOP	1/1/1949	10/31/1949	No
Midway	34.733	-88.267	180	COOP	7/1/1948	3/31/1962	No
Monsanto	35.667	-87.117	192	COOP	8/1/1948	8/31/1976	No
Mount Pleasant	35.533	-87.200	186	COOP	1/1/1949	6/30/1955	No
Mount Pleasant 1 N	35.557	-87.202	237	COOP	1/1/1953	Present	No
Muscle Shoals Regl. Arpt.	34.744	-87.600	165	COOP	2/1/1939	Present	No
Nashville	36.162	-86.772	168	COOP	9/1/1872	1/15/2003	No
Nashville Berry Field	36.108	-86.683	171	COOP	2/1/1999	Present	No
Nashville Intl. Arpt.	36.119	-86.689	183	COOP	12/1/1928	Present	No
Nashville Shelby Park	36.171	-86.736	152	COOP	9/5/2003	Present	No
Natchez	31.589	-91.341	59	COOP	9/1/1892	Present	No
Neapolis Exp. Stn.	35.720	-86.982	213	COOP	1/1/1952	Present	No
New Wilson Lock	34.817	-87.633	177	COOP	1/1/1958	6/30/1959	No
Newport	32.937	-89.759	79	COOP	M	Present	No
Oakley Exp. Stn.	32.206	-90.513	62	COOP	7/1/1948	Present	No
Ofahoma	32.764	-89.699	122	COOP	5/19/1940	3/31/2001	No
Ofahoma 2 SE	32.706	-89.672	95	COOP	10/1/1962	9/2/2003	No
Okolona	34.000	-88.750	98	COOP	1/1/1893	12/31/1986	No
Olivehill	35.267	-88.033	165	COOP	12/1/1960	3/31/1962	No
Ovilla	35.317	-87.567	296	COOP	1/1/1949	3/31/1962	No
Paden	34.667	-88.267	0	COOP	12/1/1937	11/30/1941	No
Pelahatchie	32.316	-89.799	113	COOP	11/1/1936	1/1/2001	No
Pinewood	35.900	-87.467	159	COOP	9/1/1906	3/31/1962	No
Pleasantville	35.700	-87.733	153	COOP	1/1/1949	3/31/1962	No
Point Pleasant	32.083	-91.100	24	COOP	2/1/1872	3/31/1889	No
Pontotoc	34.255	-88.993	153	COOP	12/1/1892	Present	No
Pontotoc 8 E	34.233	-88.867	116	COOP	10/1/1972	9/20/1974	No
Pontotoc Exp. Stn.	34.138	-88.998	123	COOP	5/1/1953	Present	No
Port Gibson 1 NE	31.985	-90.972	37	COOP	12/1/1893	Present	No
Red Bay	34.433	-88.133	207	COOP	1/1/1949	11/26/1979	No
Riverton	34.833	-88.333	110	COOP	10/1/1903	12/31/1938	No
Rose Hill	32.367	-90.833	0	COOP	5/1/1933	4/30/1936	No
Ross Barnett Coal Bl.	32.591	-89.780	98	COOP	2/26/1981	7/2/1998	No
Ross Barnett Res.	32.398	-90.065	94	COOP	1/1/1971	Present	No
Roxie	31.500	-91.067	0	COOP	4/16/1948	3/31/1952	No
Rural Hill	33.067	-89.283	0	COOP	5/23/1940	12/31/1950	No
Russum	31.883	-91.000	0	COOP	6/1/1948	1/31/1951	No
Shady Grove	35.750	-87.283	168	COOP	9/1/1948	10/31/1980	No
Sheffield TVA Nursery	34.767	-87.700	156	COOP	3/1/1935	7/31/1954	No
Shoccoe	32.600	-89.917	110	COOP	6/1/1900	12/31/1915	No
Smithsonia	34.767	-87.850	153	COOP	1/1/1949	4/30/1949	No

Natchez Trace Parkway – NATR

Name	Lat.	Lon.	Elev. (m)	Network	Start	End	In Park?
South Nashville	36.167	-86.717	131	COOP	1/1/1949	3/31/1962	No
St. Joseph 3 N	31.950	-91.234	24	COOP	2/1/1894	Present	No
Stonington	31.767	-91.017	58	COOP	8/1/1893	1/31/1908	No
Sugar Hill	35.533	-87.817	162	COOP	9/1/1948	9/1/1976	No
Thompson Stn.	35.774	-86.923	232	COOP	8/15/2001	Present	No
Tishomingo	34.633	-88.233	162	COOP	7/1/1944	7/31/1959	No
Tupelo	34.250	-88.717	85	COOP	1/1/1930	4/30/1969	No
Tupelo 2	34.265	-88.766	107	COOP	3/1/1998	Present	No
Tupelo 2 N	34.283	-88.717	76	COOP	11/1/1968	10/1/1983	No
Tupelo 3	34.236	-88.695	79	COOP	3/1/1998	Present	No
Tupelo Regl. Arpt.	34.262	-88.771	110	COOP	11/1/1962	Present	No
Tupelo Substn.	34.267	-88.700	79	COOP	1/1/1949	3/31/1962	No
Tuscumbia	34.717	-87.717	149	COOP	4/1/1882	3/31/1940	No
Utica	32.100	-90.633	85	COOP	7/21/1903	6/30/1970	No
Vaiden 1 SSW	33.325	-89.754	123	COOP	1/1/1893	Present	No
Van Vleet 1 SE	33.976	-88.886	101	COOP	5/1/1943	Present	No
Verona Exp. Stn.	34.204	-88.720	99	COOP	9/1/1986	Present	No
Vicksburg	32.314	-90.905	14	COOP	1/1/1892	4/25/2002	No
Vicksburg	32.350	-90.883	90	COOP	8/1/1872	6/30/1967	No
Vicksburg	32.233	-90.933	31	COOP	6/1/1950	Present	No
Vicksburg City	32.385	-90.875	24	COOP	4/1/1969	Present	No
Vicksburg Military P.	32.357	-90.844	78	COOP	7/1/1967	2/1/2004	No
Vicksburg Old	32.400	-90.783	37	COOP	7/1/1935	9/30/1950	No
Vicksburg Waterways	32.298	-90.866	55	COOP	M	11/30/2004	No
Victory	35.083	-87.817	296	COOP	9/1/1948	10/31/1980	No
Vidalia Natchez	31.533	-91.433	15	COOP	11/1/1952	2/1/1996	No
Vidalia No. 2	31.565	-91.433	18	COOP	10/30/1952	Present	No
Walnut Grove 2	32.588	-89.464	101	COOP	11/1/1962	12/2/1999	No
Walnut Grove 2 S	32.569	-89.468	110	COOP	7/1/1938	Present	No
Warner Park	36.061	-86.906	190	COOP	9/20/2000	Present	No
Waterloo	34.917	-88.067	140	COOP	7/27/1922	10/5/1976	No
Waynesboro	35.304	-87.759	229	COOP	8/1/1891	Present	No
Waynesboro 5 NW	35.350	-87.833	262	COOP	1/1/1949	7/31/1953	No
Weir	33.267	-89.300	0	COOP	6/1/1948	10/31/1948	No
West	33.194	-89.771	76	COOP	8/1/1971	4/25/2002	No
Wilson Dam	34.800	-87.617	162	COOP	1/1/1899	3/31/1962	No
Winona 5 E	33.485	-89.624	119	COOP	1/1/1953	Present	No
Woodland	33.783	-89.033	101	COOP	5/1/1909	9/30/1913	No
Youngs Store	34.950	-87.867	226	COOP	1/1/1949	3/31/1962	No
Zama	32.967	-89.383	0	COOP	8/1/1948	1/31/1957	No
AA5ED-10 Brandon	32.330	-89.978	122	CWOP	M	Present	No
AB5WF-1 Jackson	32.381	-90.113	89	CWOP	M	Present	No

Natchez Trace Parkway – NATR

Name	Lat.	Lon.	Elev. (m)	Network	Start	End	In Park?
AG4FW White Bluff	36.118	-87.228	245	CWOP	M	Present	No
CW0168 Florence	34.916	-87.860	195	CWOP	M	Present	No
CW0456 Brandon	32.359	-89.971	97	CWOP	M	Present	No
CW0815 Pegram	36.100	-87.037	235	CWOP	M	Present	No
CW2449 Sherman	34.344	-88.797	110	CWOP	M	Present	No
CW2617 Franklin	35.875	-86.844	216	CWOP	M	Present	No
CW2972 Spring Hill	35.780	-86.920	200	CWOP	M	Present	No
CW3047 Florence	34.853	-87.695	180	CWOP	M	Present	No
CW3081 Kingston Springs	36.066	-87.154	209	CWOP	M	Present	No
CW3232 Spring Hill	35.776	-86.924	241	CWOP	M	Present	No
CW3691 Canton	32.600	-89.992	88	CWOP	M	Present	No
CW4735 Florence	34.854	-87.649	183	CWOP	M	Present	No
CW5209 Kingston Springs	36.070	-87.133	237	CWOP	M	Present	No
KB5NMB-12 Fulton	34.236	-88.674	79	CWOP	M	Present	No
KB5NMB-15 Belmont	34.535	-88.167	156	CWOP	M	Present	No
KB5NMB-3 Fulton	34.275	-88.413	92	CWOP	M	Present	No
KB5NMB-5 Fulton	34.271	-88.406	104	CWOP	M	Present	No
KD4PMP Nashville	36.085	-86.938	189	CWOP	M	Present	No
KG4HDZ White Bluff	36.109	-87.237	262	CWOP	M	Present	No
KM5GE Jackson	32.341	-90.126	81	CWOP	M	Present	No
KQ4TV-4 Burns	36.049	-87.277	211	CWOP	M	Present	No
KU4WW Cherokee	34.691	-88.110	189	CWOP	M	Present	No
W4EMS Brentwood	35.990	-86.787	207	CWOP	M	Present	No
Okolona	34.090	-88.860	131	GPS-MET	M	Present	No
Vicksburg	32.330	-90.920	36	GPS-MET	M	Present	No
Clinton	32.307	-90.319	86	NADP	7/10/1984	Present	No
Burns	36.065	-87.283	215	RAWS	10/1/2003	Present	No
Delta Rd.	32.810	-90.000	28	RAWS	6/1/2002	Present	No
Meriwether Lewis	35.321	-87.458	262	RAWS	5/1/1997	Present	No
Tishomingo	34.789	-88.218	91	RAWS	8/1/2004	Present	No
Tombigbee	33.281	-89.139	168	RAWS	11/1/2003	Present	No
Warren	32.356	-90.844	76	RAWS	1/1/2004	Present	No
Jackson Hawkins Field	32.337	-90.221	104	SAO	9/1/1942	Present	No
Jackson Intl. Arpt.	32.321	-90.078	101	SAO	7/1/1963	Present	No
Muscle Shoals Regl. Arpt.	34.744	-87.600	165	SAO	2/1/1939	Present	No
Nashville Intl Arpt.	36.119	-86.689	183	SAO	12/1/1928	Present	No
Natchez Adam-Co. Arpt.	31.617	-91.283	83	SAO	1/1/1951	Present	No
Tupelo	34.250	-88.717	85	SAO	1/1/1930	4/30/1969	No
Tupelo Regl. Arpt.	34.262	-88.771	110	SAO	11/1/1962	Present	No
Vicksburg	32.233	-90.933	31	SAO	6/1/1950	Present	No
Starkville	33.630	-88.770	104	SCAN	M	Present	No
Berry Field AF	36.117	-86.683	185	WBAN	6/1/1951	10/31/1951	No

Natchez Trace Parkway – NATR							
Name	Lat.	Lon.	Elev. (m)	Network	Start	End	In Park?
Florence	34.800	-87.650	183	WBAN	3/1/1913	12/31/1940	No
Graham	35.883	-87.483	163	WBAN	7/1/1950	12/31/1951	No
Franklin	35.910	-86.880	210	WX4U	M	Present	No
Franklin	35.920	-86.870	206	WX4U	M	Present	No
WJTV Studios Jackson	32.300	-90.180	90	WX4U	M	Present	No

Two active COOP stations identified for NATR share the longest data record, starting in August 1891 (Table 4.5). Both of these stations are located in Tennessee (Figure 4.3). The COOP station "Franklin Sewage Plant" is 10 km from NATR in Franklin, Tennessee. This station has a very complete data record. The COOP station "Waynesboro" is 9 km from NATR in Waynesboro, Tennessee. This station has a very complete data record with the exception of scattered data gaps in the 1930s and 1940s. Besides the above two stations, there are several COOP stations identified for NATR, with data records starting from the 1890s, whose records are very complete, with very few or no significant data gaps. The COOP station "Natchez" (1892-present) is 3 km from NATR in southwest Mississippi. "St. Joseph 3 N" (1894-present) is a COOP station located in Louisiana, about 20 km from NATR. The COOP station "Natchez" (1893-present) is 2 km from NATR in southwest Mississippi. The COOP station "Vaiden 1 SSW" is 30 km from NATR in central Mississippi. This station measures precipitation only. The COOP station "Booneville" is 24 km from NATR in northeast Mississippi. The COOP station "Fulton 3 W" is 21 km from NATR, also in northeast Mississippi. Up until May 1956, "Fulton 3 W" measured precipitation only.

The remaining active COOP stations identified for NATR that have data records starting from the 1890s have significant data gaps. The COOP station "Canton 4 N" (1892-present) is 17 km from NATR in central Mississippi. Significant gaps occurred at this station from January 1991 to April 1994 and from September 1998 to October 1999. The COOP station "Kosciusko" (1893-present), also in central Mississippi, is only 2 km from NATR. Significant gaps occurred at this station from August 1987 to July 1989 and from January to June in 1996. In northeastern Mississippi, the COOP station "Pontotoc" (1892-present) is 20 km from NATR and has significant data gaps particularly in temperatures. No temperature observations have been taken at this site since November 1972. Precipitation observations at "Pontotoc" had a large gap between November 1972 and September 1974.

The NADP station "Clinton" is 5 km from NATR, near Jackson, Mississippi (Figure 4.3). This station has been active since 1984. A SCAN station (Starkville) is located 26 km from NATR in eastern Mississippi. In addition, there are several weather networks that provide near-real-time data within 30 km of NATR, including CWOP, RAWS, SAO, and WX4U.

Figure 4.3. Station locations for NATR.

Six active RAWS stations have been identified within 30 km of NATR (Table 4.5). The RAWS station with the longest record is "Meriwether Lewis," located 9 km from NATR in southern Tennessee (Figure 4.3). This is also the closest RAWS station to NATR among these six RAWS sites. One other RAWS station (Burns) is also located in Tennessee, while the remaining stations are located in Mississippi.

Several SAO stations are located within 30 km of NATR (Table 4.5). The closest SAO stations ("Natchez Adam-Co. Arpt." in southwest Mississippi and "Tupelo Regl. Arpt." in northeast Mississippi) are less than a kilometer from NATR. The SAO station with the longest record is "Nashville Intl. Arpt.." 29 km east of the northern terminus of NATR (Figure 4.3).

5.0. Conclusions and Recommendations

We have based our findings on an examination of available climate records within GULN units, discussions with NPS staff and other collaborators, and prior knowledge of the area. Here, we offer an evaluation and general comments pertaining to the status, prospects, and needs for climate-monitoring capabilities in GULN.

5.1. Gulf Coast Inventory and Monitoring Network

Two park units within the GULN have areas of little or no weather/climate station coverage that could be addressed. Padre Island National Seashore (PAIS) currently has no coverage within the main portion of Padre Island, nor are there any available stations at inland locations to the west of the park unit. Almost all of the available weather/climate stations are located within 30 km of either the north tip of PAIS (Corpus Christi area) or at the south tip of PAIS (Port Mansfield and nearby communities). The six stations identified for GUIS are all in the eastern portions of GULN, along the Florida Panhandle; the western islands of GUIS have no stations on them. There are still plenty of weather and climate stations along the Mississippi coast that can provide data for the western island units of GUIS; however, this does not help in monitoring local conditions at the islands themselves.

Two parks units in the GULN, PAAL and SAAN, have no weather/climate stations within their park boundaries. These park units must rely heavily on outside sources of weather and climate data. This station coverage of both long-term and near-real-time stations is fortunately available for both PAAL and SAAN.

A few of the parks units of the GULN have anywhere from one to at most a few weather and/or climate stations within the park unit. These park units include BITH, JELA, and VICK. Despite having these valuable stations, the park units in this category must still rely heavily on outside sources of weather and climate data. For all three of these park units, we have deemed the coverage outside the park units of both near-real-time weather stations and long-term climate stations to be satisfactory to address the weather- and climate-monitoring objectives laid out by the GULN. The expansion of weather-monitoring efforts at BITH could be considered, as it is comprised of several units, only one of which currently has any ongoing weather monitoring (Turkey Creek unit: one RAWS station). Since the RAWS network already has a presence in the BITH region, NPS may benefit by considering working with local officials to install additional RAWS stations at other BITH units.

5.2. Spatial Variations in Mean Climate

Land-use heterogeneity, particularly land uses introduced by human settlement, influences heavily the park units within GULN, leading to systematic spatial variations in mean surface climate. This is true at local scales in particular; with local variations over short horizontal distances, land use patterns introduce considerable fine-scale structure to mean climate (temperature and precipitation). Sharp coastal-interior temperature gradients and resulting precipitation patterns can also be important for the GULN park units, particularly in summer months where convective precipitation events associated with land-sea breezes become more common. Issues encountered in mapping mean climate are discussed in Appendix D and in Redmond et al. (2005).

If only a few stations will be emplaced in a previously-unsampled area, the primary goal should be overall characterization of the main climate elements (temperature and precipitation, and snow). This level of characterization generally requires that the stations should be distributed spatially in the major biomes of each park, located in those land uses/land covers that most truly represent the local area. If such stations already are present in the vicinity, then additional stations would be best used for two important and somewhat competing purposes: (a) add redundancy as backup for loss of data from current stations (or loss of the physical stations) or (b) provide added information on spatial heterogeneity in climate arising from land use variations, particularly local wind patterns.

5.3. Climate Change Detection

There is much interest in the adaptation of GULN ecosystems in response to possible future climate change. This particularly includes climate influences from land use changes and possible impacts of sea-level rises on coastal ecosystems, and the introduction of non-native plant and animal communities.

The desire for credible, accurate, complete, and long-term climate records—from any location— cannot be overemphasized. Thus, this consideration always should have a high priority. However, because of spatial diversity in climate, monitoring that fills knowledge gaps and provides information on long-term temporal variability in short-distance relationships also will be valuable. We cannot be sure that climate variability and climate change will affect all parts of a given park unit equally. In fact, it is appropriate to speculate that this is not the case, and spatial variations in temporal variability extend to small spatial scales, a consequence of diversity within GULN in land use patterns.

5.4. Aesthetics

This issue arises frequently enough to deserve comment. Standards for quality climate measurements require open exposures away from heat sources, buildings, pavement, close vegetation and tall trees, and human intrusion (thus away from property lines). By their nature, sites that meet these standards are usually quite visible. In many settings (such as heavily forested areas) these sites also are quite rare, making them precisely the same places that managers wish to protect from aesthetic intrusion. The most suitable and scientifically defensible sites frequently are rejected as candidate locations for weather/climate stations. Most weather/climate stations, therefore, tend to be "hidden" but many of these hidden locations have inferior exposures. Some measure of compromise is nearly always called for in siting weather and climate stations.

The public has vast interest and curiosity in weather and climate, and within the NPS I&M networks, such measurements consistently rate near or at the top of desired public information. There seem to be many possible opportunities for exploiting and embracing this widespread interest within the interpretive mission of the NPS. One way to do this would be to highlight rather than hide these stations and educate the public about the need for adequate siting. A number of weather displays we have encountered during visits have proven inadvertently to serve as counterexamples for how measurements should not be made.

5.5. Information Access

Access to information promotes its use, which in turn promotes attention to station care and maintenance, better data, and more use. An end-to-end view that extends from sensing to decision support is far preferable to isolated and disconnected activities and aids the support infrastructure that is ultimately so necessary for successful, long-term climate monitoring.

Decisions about improvements in monitoring capacity are facilitated greatly by the ability to examine available climate information. Various methods are being created at WRCC to improve access to that information. Web pages providing historic and ongoing climate data, and information from GULN park units can be accessed at http://www.wrcc.dri.edu/nps. In the event that this URL changes, there still will be links from the main WRCC Web page entitled "Projects" under NPS.

The WRCC has been steadily developing software to summarize data from hourly sites. This has been occurring under the aegis of the RAWS program and a growing array of product generators ranging from daily and monthly data lists to wind roses and hourly frequency distributions. All park data are available to park personnel via an access code (needed only for data listings) that can be acquired by request. The WRCC RAWS Web page is located at http://www.wrcc.dri.edu/wraws or http://www.raws.dri.edu.

Web pages have been developed to provide access not only to historic and ongoing climate data and information from GULN park units but also to climate-monitoring efforts for GULN. These pages can be found through http://www.wrcc.dri.edu/nps.

Additional access to more standard climate information is accessible though the previously mentioned Web pages, as well as through http://www.wrcc.dri.edu/summary. These summaries are generally for COOP stations.

5.6. Summarized Conclusions and Recommendations

- NPS could benefit by addressing the lack of weather/climate station coverage at both PAIS and western islands of GUIS. This is particularly valuable in light of the emphasis on monitoring coastal dynamics and responses to future climate changes within coastal park units of GULN.
- Although several GULN park units have none to at most a few weather/climate stations within their boundaries, most of these park units have generally satisfactory station coverage available within 30 km of their boundaries.
- With the exception of the Turkey Creek unit of BITH (one RAWS station), most BITH units have no weather/climate stations inside their boundaries. Since the RAWS network already is present within BITH, NPS may consider adding additional RAWS stations in other BITH units.

6.0. Literature Cited

American Association of State Climatologists. 1985. Heights and exposure standards for sensors on automated weather stations. The State Climatologist **9**.

Bevis, M., S. Businger, T. A. Herring, C. Rocken, R. A. Anthes, and R. H. Ware. 1992. GPS meteorology: remote sensing of the atmospheric water vapor using the global positioning system. Journal of Geophysical Research **97**:75–94.

Bonan, G. B. 2002. Ecological Climatology: Concepts and Applications. Cambridge University Press.

Bove, M. C., D. F. Zierden, and J. J. O'Brien. 1998. Are Gulf landfalling hurricanes getting stronger? Bulletin of the American Meteorological Society **79**:1327-1328.

Bruce, K. A., G. N. Cameron, and P. A. Harcombe. 1995. Initiation of a new woodland type on the Texas coastal prairie by the Chinese tallow tree (Sapium sebiferum (L.) Roxb.). Bulletin of the Torrey Botanical Club **122**:215–225.

Bureau of Land Management. 1997. Remote Automatic Weather Station (RAWS) and Remote Environmental Monitoring Systems (REMS) standards. RAWS/REMS Support Facility, Boise, Idaho.

Chapin III, F. S., M. S. Torn, and M. Tateno. 1996. Principles of ecosystem sustainability. The American Naturalist **148**:1016-1037.

Cooter, E. J., M. B. Richman, P. J. Lamb, and D. A. Sampson. 2000. A climate change database for biological assessments in the southeastern United States: Development and case study. Climatic Change **44**:89–121.

Daly, C., R. P. Neilson, and D. L. Phillips. 1994. A statistical-topographic model for mapping climatological precipitation over mountainous terrain. Journal of Applied Meteorology **33**:140-158.

Daly, C., W. P. Gibson, G. H. Taylor, G. L. Johnson, and P. Pasteris. 2002. A knowledge-based approach to the statistical mapping of climate. Climate Research **22**:99-113.

Doggett, M., C. Daly, J. Smith, W. Gibson, G. Taylor, G. Johnson, and P. Pasteris. 2004. High-resolution 1971-2000 mean monthly temperature maps for the western United States. Fourteenth AMS Conf. on Applied Climatology, 84th AMS Annual Meeting. Seattle, Washington, American Meteorological Society, Boston, Massachusetts, January 2004, Paper 4.3, CD-ROM.

Duan, J., M. Bevis, P. Fang, Y. Bock, S. Chiswell, S. Businger, C. Rocken, F. Solheim, T. van Hove, R. Ware, and others. 1996. GPS meteorology: direct estimation of the absolute value of precipitable water. Journal of Applied Meteorology **35**:830-838.

Environmental Protection Agency. 1987. On-site meteorological program guidance for regulatory modeling applications. EPA-450/4-87-013. Environmental Protection Agency, Office of Air Quality Planning and Standards, Research Triangle Park, North Carolina.

Finklin, A. I., and W. C. Fischer. 1990. Weather station handbook –an interagency guide for wildland managers. NFES No. 2140. National Wildfire Coordinating Group, Boise, Idaho.

Gibson, W. P., C. Daly, T. Kittel, D. Nychka, C. Johns, N. Rosenbloom, A. McNab, and G. Taylor. 2002. Development of a 103-year high-resolution climate data set for the conterminous United States. Thirteenth AMS Conf. on Applied Climatology. Portland, Oregon, American Meteorological Society, Boston, Massachusetts, May 2002:181-183.

Goldenberg, S. B., and L. J. Shapiro. 1996. Physical mechanisms for the association of El Niño and West African rainfall with Atlantic major hurricane activity. Journal of Climate **9**:1169-1187.

Gray, W. 1984a. Atlantic seasonal hurricane frequency. Part I: El Niño and 30 mb quasi-biennial oscillation influences. Monthly Weather Review **112**:1649-1668.

Gray, W. 1984b. Atlantic seasonal hurricane frequency. Part II: Forecasting its variability. Monthly Weather Review **112**:1669-1683.

Harcombe, P. A., et al. (1998). Sensitivity of Gulf Coast forests to climate change. *In* G. R. Guntenspergen and B. A. Vairin, eds. Vulnerability of coastal wetlands in the southeastern United States: climate change research results, 1922–97. USGS/BRD/ BSR-1998-0002. U.S. Geological Survey, Biological Resources Division. Lafayette, Louisiana.

Henderson-Sellers, A., H. Zhang, G. Berz, K. Emanuel, W. Gray, C. Landsea, G. Holland, J. Lighthill, S.-L. Shieh, P. Webster, and others. 1998. Tropical cyclones and global climate change: a post-IPCC assessment. Bulletin of the American Meteorological Society **79**:19-38.

I&M. 2006. I&M Inventories home page. http://science.nature.nps.gov/im/inventory/index.cfm.

Jacobson, M. C., R. J. Charlson, H. Rodhe, and G. H. Orians. 2000. Earth System Science: From Biogeochemical Cycles to Global Change. Academic Press, San Diego.

Justic, D., N. N. Rabalais, and R. E. Turner. 1996. Effects of climate change on hypoxia in coastal waters: A doubled CO_2 scenario for the northern Gulf of Mexico. Limnology and Oceanography **41**:992–1003.

Karl, T. R., V. E. Derr, D. R. Easterling, C. K. Folland, D. J. Hoffman, S. Levitus, N. Nicholls, D. E. Parker, and G. W. Withee. 1996. Critical issues for long-term climate monitoring. Pages 55-92 *in* T. R. Karl, editor. Long Term Climate Monitoring by the Global Climate Observing System, Kluwer Publishing.

Lyons, S. W. 2004. U.S. tropical cyclone landfall variability: 1950-2002. Weather and Forecasting **19**:473-480.

Miller, J. R., and G. L. Russel. 1992. The impact of global warming on river runoff. Journal of Geophysical Research **97**:2757–2764.

Mulholland, P. J., G. R. Best, C. C. Coutant, G. M. Hornberger, J. L. Meyer, P. J. Robinson, J. R. Stenberg, R. E. Turner, F. Vera-Herrera, and R. G. Wetzel. 1997. Effects of climate change on freshwater ecosystems of the southeastern United States and the Gulf of Mexico. Hydrological Processes **11**:949–970.

National Assessment Synthesis Team. 2001. Climate Change Impacts on the United States: The Potential Consequences of Climate Variability and Change, Report for the U.S. Global Change Research Program. Cambridge University Press, Cambridge, UK.

National Research Council. 2001. A Climate Services Vision: First Steps Toward the Future. National Academies Press, Washington, D.C.

National Wildfire Coordinating Group. 2004. National fire danger rating system weather station standards. Report PMS 426.3. National Wildfire Coordinating Group, Boise, Idaho.

Neilson, R. P. 1987. Biotic regionalization and climatic controls in western North America. Vegetatio **70**:135-147.

Ning, Z. H., and K. Abdollahi. 1999. Global climate change and its consequences on the Gulf Coast Region of the United States.Franklin Press and Gulf Coast Regional Climate Change Council. Baton Rouge, Louisiana. Available from www.nacc.usgcrp.gov/regions/gulfcoast/workshop-report.html. (accessed 1 December 2006).

Oakley, K. L., L. P. Thomas, and S. G. Fancy. 2003. Guidelines for long-term monitoring protocols. Wildlife Society Bulletin **31**:1000-1003.

Penland, S., and K. E. Ramsey. 1990. Relative sea level rise in Louisiana and the Gulf of Mexico: 1908–1988. Journal of Coastal Research **6**:323–342.

Redmond, K. T., D. B. Simeral, and G. D. McCurdy. 2005. Climate monitoring for southwest Alaska national parks: network design and site selection. Report 05-01. Western Regional Climate Center, Reno, Nevada.

Reid, W. V., and M. C. Trexler. 1992. Responding to potential impacts of climate change on U.S. coastal biodiversity. Coastal Management **20**:117–142.

Schlesinger, W. H. 1997. Biogeochemistry: An Analysis of Global Change. Academic Press, San Diego.

Segura, M., W. Granger, M. Byrne, and L. German. 2005. Gulf Coast Network vital signs monitoring plan - Phase II (draft) Report. National Park Service, Gulf Coast Network, Lafayette, Louisiana.

Smith, E. 1999. Atlantic and East Coast hurricanes 1900-98: a frequency and intensity study for the twenty-first century. Bulletin of the American Meteorological Society **80**:2717-2720.

Stone, G. W., P. Wang, D. A. Pepper, J. M. Grymes III, H. H. Roberts, X. Zhang, S. A. Hsu, and O. K. Huh. 1999. Studying the importance of hurricanes to the northern Gulf of Mexico coast. EOS Transactions, American Geophysical Union **80**:301–305.

Tanner, B. D. 1990. Automated weather stations. Remote Sensing Reviews **5**:73-98.

Trenberth, K.E. 2005. Uncertainty in hurricanes and global warming. Science **308**:1753-1754.

Twilley, R. R., E. J. Barron, H. L. Gholz, M. A. Harwell, R. L. Miller, D. J. Reed, J. B. Rose, E. H. Siemann, R. G. Wetzel, and R. J. Zimmerman. 2001. Confronting climate change in the Gulf Coast region: prospects for sustaining our ecological heritage. Union of Concerned Scientists, Cambridge, MA, and Ecological Society of America, Washington, D.C.

Twilley, R. R. and V. Rivera-Monroy. 2005. Conceptual ecological model development for the National Park Service units of the Gulf Coast Network. Unpublished Report prepared for the USDI National Park Service Gulf Coast Network. 94pp.

World Meteorological Organization. 1983. Guide to meteorological instruments and methods of observation, No. 8, 5th edition, World Meteorological Organization, Geneva Switzerland.

World Meteorological Organization. 2005. Organization and planning of intercomparisons of rainfall intensity gauges. World Meteorological Organization, Geneva Switzerland.

Yuan, L. L., R. A. Anthes, R. H. Ware, C. Rocken, W. D. Bonner, M. G. Bevis, and S. Businger. 1993. Sensing climate change using the global positioning system. Journal of Geophysical Research **98**:14925-14937.

Appendix A. Glossary

Climate—Complete and entire ensemble of statistical descriptors of temporal and spatial properties comprising the behavior of the atmosphere. These descriptors include means, variances, frequency distributions, autocorrelations, spatial correlations and other patterns of association, temporal lags, and element-to-element relationships. The descriptors have a physical basis in flows and reservoirs of energy and mass. Climate and weather phenomena shade gradually into each other and are ultimately inseparable.

Climate Element—(same as Weather Element) Attribute or property of the state of the atmosphere that is measured, estimated, or derived. Examples of climate elements include temperature, wind speed, wind direction, precipitation amount, precipitation type, relative humidity, dewpoint, solar radiation, snow depth, soil temperature at a given depth, etc. A derived element is a function of other elements (like degree days or number of days with rain) and is not measured directly with a sensor. The terms "parameter" or "variable" are not used to describe elements.

Climate Network—Group of climate stations having a common purpose; the group is often owned and maintained by a single organization.

Climate Station—Station where data are collected to track atmospheric conditions over the long-term. Often, this station operates to additional standards to verify long-term consistency. For these stations, the detailed circumstances surrounding a set of measurements (siting and exposure, instrument changes, etc.) are important.

Data—Measurements specifying the state of the physical environment. Does not include metadata.

Data Inventory—Information about overall data properties for each station within a weather or climate network. A data inventory may include start/stop dates, percentages of available data, breakdowns by climate element, counts of actual data values, counts or fractions of data types, etc. These properties must be determined by actually reading the data and thus require the data to be available, accessible, and in a readable format.

NPS I&M Network—A set of NPS park units grouped by a common theme, typically by natural resource and/or geographic region.

Metadata—Information necessary to interpret environmental data properly, organized as a history or series of snapshots—data about data. Examples include details of measurement processes, station circumstances and exposures, assumptions about the site, network purpose and background, types of observations and sensors, pre-treatment of data, access information, maintenance history and protocols, observational methods, archive locations, owner, and station start/end period.

Quality Assurance—Planned and systematic set of activities to provide adequate confidence that products and services are resulting in credible and correct information. Includes quality control.

Quality Control—Evaluation, assessment, and improvement of imperfect data by utilizing other imperfect data.

Station Inventory—Information about a set of stations obtained from metadata that accompany the network or networks. A station inventory can be compiled from direct and indirect reports prepared by others.

Weather—Instantaneous state of the atmosphere at any given time, mainly with respect to its effects on biological activities. As distinguished from climate, weather consists of the short-term (minutes to days) variations in the atmosphere. Popularly, weather is thought of in terms of temperature, precipitation, humidity, wind, sky condition, visibility, and cloud conditions.

Weather Element (same as Climate Element)—Attribute or property of the state of the atmosphere that is measured, estimated, or derived. Examples of weather elements include temperature, wind speed, wind direction, precipitation amount, precipitation type, relative humidity, dewpoint, solar radiation, snow depth, soil temperature at a given depth, etc. A derived weather element is a function of other elements (like degree days or number of days with rain) and is not measured directly. The terms "parameter" and "variable" are not used to describe weather elements.

Weather Network—Group of weather stations usually owned and maintained by a particular organization and usually for a specific purpose.

Weather Station—Station where collected data are intended for near-real-time use with less need for reference to long-term conditions. In many cases, the detailed circumstances of a set of measurements (siting and exposure, instrument changes, etc.) from weather stations are not as important as for climate stations.

Appendix B. Climate-monitoring principles

Since the late 1990s, frequent references have been made to a set of climate-monitoring principles enunciated in 1996 by Tom Karl, director of the NOAA NCDC in Asheville, North Carolina. These monitoring principles also have been referred to informally as the "Ten Commandments of Climate Monitoring." Both versions are given here. In addition, these principles have been adopted by the Global Climate Observing System (GCOS 2004).

(Compiled by Kelly Redmond, Western Regional Climate Center, Desert Research Institute, August 2000.)

B.1. Full Version (Karl et al. 1996)

B.1.1. Effects on climate records of instrument changes, observing practices, observation locations, sampling rates, etc., must be known before such changes are implemented. This can be ascertained through a period where overlapping measurements from old and new observing systems are collected or sometimes by comparing the old and new observing systems with a reference standard. Site stability for in situ measurements, both in terms of physical location and changes in the nearby environment, also should be a key criterion in site selection. Thus, many synoptic network stations, which are primarily used in weather forecasting but also provide valuable climate data, and dedicated climate stations intended to be operational for extended periods must be subject to this policy.

B.1.2. Processing algorithms and changes in these algorithms must be well documented. Documentation should be carried with the data throughout the data-archiving process.

B.1.3. Knowledge of instrument, station, and/or platform history is essential for interpreting and using the data. Changes in instrument sampling time, local environmental conditions for in situ measurements, and other factors pertinent to interpreting the observations and measurements should be recorded as a mandatory part in the observing routine and be archived with the original data.

B.1.4. In situ and other observations with a long, uninterrupted record should be maintained. Every effort should be applied to protect the data sets that have provided long-term, homogeneous observations. "Long-term" for space-based measurements is measured in decades, but for more conventional measurements, "long-term" may be a century or more. Each element in the observational system should develop a list of prioritized sites or observations based on their contribution to long-term climate monitoring.

B.1.5. Calibration, validation, and maintenance facilities are critical requirements for long-term climatic data sets. Homogeneity in the climate record must be assessed routinely, and corrective action must become part of the archived record.

B.1.6. Where feasible, some level of "low-technology" backup to "high-technology" observing systems should be developed to safeguard against unexpected operational failures.

B.1.7. Regions having insufficient data, variables and regions sensitive to change, and key measurements lacking adequate spatial and temporal resolution should be given the highest priority in designing and implementing new climate-observing systems.

B.1.8. Network designers and instrument engineers must receive long-term climate requirements at the outset of the network design process. This is particularly important because most observing systems have been designed for purposes other than long-term climate monitoring. Instruments must possess adequate accuracy with biases small enough to document climate variations and changes.

B.1.9. Much of the development of new observational capabilities and the evidence supporting the value of these observations stem from research-oriented needs or programs. A lack of stable, long-term commitment to these observations and lack of a clear transition plan from research to operations are two frequent limitations in the development of adequate, long-term monitoring capabilities. Difficulties in securing a long-term commitment must be overcome in order to improve the climate-observing system in a timely manner with minimal interruptions.

B.1.10. Data management systems that facilitate access, use, and interpretation are essential. Freedom of access, low cost, mechanisms that facilitate use (directories, catalogs, browse capabilities, availability of metadata on station histories, algorithm accessibility and documentation, etc.) and quality control should guide data management. International cooperation is critical for successful management of data used to monitor long-term climate change and variability.

B.2. Abbreviated version, "Ten Commandments of Climate Monitoring"

B.2.1. Assess the impact of new climate-observing systems or changes to existing systems before they are implemented.

"Thou shalt properly manage network change." (assess effects of proposed changes)

B.2.2. Require a suitable period where measurement from new and old climate-observing systems will overlap.

"Thou shalt conduct parallel testing." (compare old and replacement systems)

B.2.3. Treat calibration, validation, algorithm-change, and data-homogeneity assessments with the same care as the data.

"Thou shalt collect metadata." (fully document system and operating procedures)

B.2.4. Verify capability for routinely assessing the quality and homogeneity of the data including high-resolution data for extreme events.

"Thou shalt assure data quality and continuity." (assess as part of routine operating procedures)

B.2.5. Integrate assessments like those conducted by the International Panel on Climate Change into global climate-observing priorities.

"Thou shalt anticipate the use of data." (integrated environmental assessment; component in operational plan for system)

B.2.6. Maintain long-term weather and climate stations.

"Thou shalt worship historic significance." (maintain homogeneous data sets from long–term, climate-observing systems)

B.2.7. Place high priority on increasing observations in regions lacking sufficient data and in regions sensitive to change and variability.

"Thou shalt acquire complementary data." (new sites to fill observational gaps)

B.2.8. Provide network operators, designers, and instrument engineers with long-term requirements at the outset of the design and implementation phases for new systems.

"Thou shalt specify requirements for climate observation systems." (application and usage of observational data)

B.2.9. Carefully consider the transition from research-observing system to long-term operation.

"Thou shalt have continuity of purpose." (stable long-term commitments)

B.2.10. Focus on data-management systems that facilitate access, use, and interpretation of weather data and metadata.

"Thou shalt provide access to data and metadata." (readily available weather and climate information)

B.3. Literature Cited

Karl, T. R., V. E. Derr, D. R. Easterling, C. K. Folland, D. J. Hoffman, S. Levitus, N. Nicholls, D. E. Parker, and G. W. Withee. 1996. Critical Issues for Long-Term Climate Monitoring. Pages 55-92 *in* T. R. Karl, editor. Long Term Climate Monitoring by the Global Climate Observing System, Kluwer Publishing.

Global Climate Observing System. 2004. Implementation Plan for the Global Observing System for Climate in Support of the UNFCCC. GCOS-92, WMO/TD No. 1219, World Meteorological Organization, Geneva, Switzerland.

Appendix C. Factors in operating a climate network

C.1. Climate versus Weather
- Climate measurements require _consistency through time._

C.2. Network Purpose
- Anticipated or desired lifetime.
- Breadth of network mission (commitment by needed constituency).
- Dedicated constituency—no network survives without a dedicated constituency.

C.3. Site Identification and Selection
- Spanning gradients in climate or biomes with transects.
- Issues regarding representative spatial scale—site uniformity versus site clustering.
- Alignment with and contribution to network mission.
- Exposure—ability to measure representative quantities.
- Logistics—ability to service station (Always or only in favorable weather?).
- Site redundancy (positive for quality control, negative for extra resources).
- Power—is AC needed?
- Site security—is protection from vandalism needed?
- Permitting often a major impediment and usually underestimated.

C.4. Station Hardware
- Survival—weather is the main cause of lost weather/climate data.
- Robustness of sensors—ability to measure and record in any condition.
- Quality—distrusted records are worthless and a waste of time and money.
  - High quality—will cost up front but pays off later.
  - Low quality—may provide a lower start-up cost but will cost more later (low cost can be expensive).
- Redundancy—backup if sensors malfunction.
- Ice and snow—measurements are much more difficult than rain measurements.
- Severe environments (expense is about two–three times greater than for stations in more benign settings).

C.5. Communications
- Reliability—live data have a much larger constituency.
- One-way or two-way.
  - Retrieval of missed transmissions.
  - Ability to reprogram data logger remotely.
  - Remote troubleshooting abilities.
  - Continuing versus one-time costs.
- Back-up procedures to prevent data loss during communication outages.
- Live communications increase problems but also increase value.

C.6. Maintenance
- Main reason why networks fail (and most networks do eventually fail!).

- <u>Key</u> issue with nearly every network.
- Who will perform maintenance?
- Degree of commitment and motivation to contribute.
- Periodic? On-demand as needed? Preventive?
- Equipment change-out schedules and upgrades for sensors and software.
- Automated stations require <u>skilled</u> and <u>experienced</u> labor.
- Calibration—sensors often drift (climate).
- Site maintenance essential (constant vegetation, surface conditions, nearby influences).
- Typical automated station will cost about $2K per year to maintain.
- Documentation—photos, notes, visits, changes, essential for posterity.
- Planning for equipment life cycle and technological advances.

C.7. Maintaining Programmatic Continuity and Corporate Knowledge
- Long-term vision and commitment needed.
- Institutionalizing versus personalizing—developing appropriate dependencies.

C.8. Data Flow
- Centralized ingest?
- Centralized access to data and data products?
- Local version available?
- Contract out work or do it yourself?
- Quality control of data.
- Archival.
- Metadata—historic information, not a snapshot. Every station should collect metadata.
- Post-collection processing, multiple data-ingestion paths.

C.9. Products
- Most basic product consists of the data values.
- Summaries.
- Write own applications or leverage existing mechanisms?

C.10. Funding
- Prototype approaches as proof of concept.
- Linking and leveraging essential.
- Constituencies—every network <u>needs</u> a constituency.
- Bridging to practical and operational communities? Live data needed.
- Bridging to counterpart research efforts and initiatives—funding source.
- Creativity, resourcefulness, and persistence usually are essential to success.

C.11. Final Comments
- Deployment is by far the easiest part in operating a network.
- Maintenance is the main issue.
- Best analogy: Operating a network is like raising a child; it requires constant attention.

Source: Western Regional Climate Center (WRCC)

Appendix D. General design considerations for weather/climate-monitoring programs

The process for designing a climate-monitoring program benefits from anticipating design and protocol issues discussed here. Much of this material is been excerpted from a report addressing the Channel Islands National Park (Redmond and McCurdy 2005), where an example is found illustrating how these factors can be applied to a specific setting. Many national park units possess some climate or meteorology feature that sets them apart from more familiar or "standard" settings.

D.1. Introduction

There are several criteria that must be used in deciding to deploy new stations and where these new stations should be sited.

- Where are existing stations located?
- Where have data been gathered in the past (discontinued locations)?
- Where would a new station fill a knowledge gap about basic, long-term climatic averages for an area of interest?
- Where would a new station fill a knowledge gap about how climate behaves over time?
- As a special case for behavior over time, what locations might be expected to show a more sensitive response to climate change?
- How do answers to the preceding questions depend on the climate element? Are answers the same for precipitation, temperature, wind, snowfall, humidity, etc.?
- What role should manual measurements play? How should manual measurements interface with automated measurements?
- Are there special technical or management issues, either present or anticipated in the next 5–15 years, requiring added climate information?
- What unique information is provided in addition to information from existing sites? "Redundancy is bad."
- What nearby information is available to estimate missing observations because observing systems always experience gaps and lose data? "Redundancy is good."
- How would logistics and maintenance affect these decisions?

In relation to the preceding questions, there are several topics that should be considered. The following topics are not listed in a particular order.

D.1.1. Network Purpose

Humans seem to have an almost reflexive need to measure temperature and precipitation, along with other climate elements. These reasons span a broad range from utilitarian to curiosity-driven. Although there are well-known recurrent patterns of need and data use, new uses are always appearing. The number of uses ranges in the thousands. Attempts have been made to categorize such uses (see NRC 1998; NRC 2001). Because climate measurements are accumulated over a long time, they should be treated as multi-purpose and should be undertaken in a manner that serves the widest possible applications. Some applications remain constant, while others rise and fall in importance. An insistent issue today may subside, while the next pressing issue of tomorrow barely may be anticipated. The notion that humans might affect the climate of the entire Earth was nearly unimaginable when the national USDA (later NOAA) cooperative weather network began in the late 1800s. Abundant experience has shown, however, that there always will be a demand for a history record of climate measurements and their properties. Experience also shows that there is an expectation that climate measurements will be taken and made available to the general public.

An exhaustive list of uses for data would fill many pages and still be incomplete. In broad terms, however, there are needs to document environmental conditions that disrupt or otherwise affect park operations (e.g., storms and droughts). Design and construction standards are determined by climatological event frequencies that exceed certain thresholds. Climate is a determinant that sometimes attracts and sometimes discourages visitors. Climate may play a large part in the park experience (e.g., Death Valley and heat are nearly synonymous). Some park units are large enough to encompass spatial or elevation diversity in climate, and the sequence of events can vary considerably inside or close to park boundaries. That is, temporal trends and statistics may not be the same everywhere, and this spatial structure should be sampled. The granularity of this structure depends on the presence of topography or large climate gradients or both, such as that found along the U.S. West Coast in summer with the rapid transition from the marine layer to the hot interior.

Plant and animal communities and entire ecosystems react to every nuance in the physical environment. No aspect of weather and climate goes undetected in the natural world. Wilson (1998) proposed "an informal rule of biological evolution" that applies here: "If an organic sensor can be imagined that is capable of detecting any particular environmental signal, a species exists somewhere that possesses this sensor." Every weather and climate event, whether dull or extraordinary to humans, matters to some organism. Dramatic events and creeping incremental change both have consequences to living systems. Extreme events or disturbances can "reset the clock" or "shake up the system" and lead to reverberations that last for years to centuries or longer. Slow change can carry complex nonlinear systems (e.g., any living assemblage) into states where chaotic transitions and new behavior occur. These changes are seldom predictable, typically are observed after the fact, and understood only in retrospect. Climate changes may not be exciting, but as a well-known atmospheric scientist, Mike Wallace, from the University of Washington once noted, "subtle does not mean unimportant".

Thus, individuals who observe the climate should be able to record observations accurately and depict both rapid and slow changes. In particular, an array of artificial influences easily can confound detection of slow changes. The record as provided can contain both real climate variability (that took place in the atmosphere) and fake climate variability (that arose directly from the way atmospheric changes were observed and recorded). As an example, trees growing near a climate station with an excellent anemometer will make it appear that the wind gradually slowed down over many years. Great care must be taken to protect against sources of fake climate variability on the longer-time scales of years to decades. Processes leading to the observed climate are not stationary; rather these processes draw from probability distributions that vary with time. For this reason, climatic time series do not exhibit statistical stationarity. The implications are manifold. There are no true climatic "normals" to which climate inevitably must return. Rather, there are broad ranges of climatic conditions. Climate does not demonstrate exact repetition but instead continual fluctuation and sometimes approximate repetition. In addition, there is always new behavior waiting to occur. Consequently, the business of climate monitoring is never finished, and there is no point where we can state confidently that "enough" is known.

D.1.2. Robustness
The most frequent cause for loss of weather data is the weather itself, the very thing we wish to record. The design of climate and weather observing programs should consider the meteorological equivalent of "peaking power" employed by utilities. Because environmental disturbances have significant effects on ecologic systems, sensors, data loggers, and communications networks should be able to function during the most severe conditions that realistically can be anticipated over the next 50–100 years. Systems designed in this manner are less likely to fail under more ordinary conditions, as well as more likely to transmit continuous, quality data for both tranquil and active periods.

D.1.3. Weather versus Climate
For "weather" measurements, pertaining to what is approximately happening here and now, small moves and changes in exposure are not as critical. For "climate" measurements, where values from different points in time are compared, siting and exposure are critical factors, and it is vitally important that the observing circumstances remain essentially unchanged over the duration of the station record.

Station moves can affect different elements to differing degrees. Even small moves of several meters, especially vertically, can affect temperature records. Hills and knolls act differently from the bottoms of small swales, pockets, or drainage channels (Whiteman 2000; Geiger et al. 2003). Precipitation is probably less subject to change with moves of 50–100 m than other elements (that is, precipitation has less intrinsic variation in small spaces) except if wind flow over the gauge is affected.

D.1.4. Physical Setting
Siting and exposure, and their continuity and consistency through time, significantly influence the climate records produced by a station. These two terms have overlapping connotations. We use the term "siting" in a more general sense, reserving the term "exposure" generally for the particular circumstances affecting the ability of an instrument to record measurements that are representative of the desired spatial or temporal scale.

D.1.5. Measurement Intervals
Climatic processes occur continuously in time, but our measurement systems usually record in discrete chunks of time: for example, seconds, hours, or days. These measurements often are referred to as "systematic" measurements. Interval averages may hide active or interesting periods of highly intense activity. Alternatively, some systems record "events" when a certain threshold of activity is exceeded (examples: another millimeter of precipitation has fallen, another kilometer of wind has moved past, the temperature has changed by a degree, a gust higher than 9.9 m/s has been measured). When this occurs, measurements from all sensors are reported. These measurements are known as "breakpoint" data. In relatively unchanging conditions (long calm periods or rainless weeks, for example), event recorders should send a signal that they are still "alive and well." If systematic recorders are programmed to note and periodically report the highest, lowest, and mean value within each time interval, the likelihood

is reduced that interesting behavior will be glossed over or lost. With the capacity of modern data loggers, it is recommended to record and report extremes within the basic time increment (e.g., hourly or 10 minutes). This approach also assists quality-control procedures.

There is usually a trade-off between data volume and time increment, and most automated systems now are set to record approximately hourly. A number of field stations maintained by WRCC are programmed to record in 5- or 10-minute increments, which readily serve to construct an hourly value. However, this approach produces 6–12 times as much data as hourly data. These systems typically do not record details of events at sub-interval time scales, but they easily can record peak values, or counts of threshold exceedance, within the time intervals.

Thus, for each time interval at an automated station, we recommend that several kinds of information—mean or sum, extreme maximum and minimum, and sometimes standard deviation—be recorded. These measurements are useful for quality control and other purposes. Modern data loggers and office computers have quite high capacity. Diagnostic information indicating the state of solar chargers or battery voltages and their extremes is of great value. This topic will be discussed in greater detail in a succeeding section.

Automation also has made possible adaptive or intelligent monitoring techniques where systems vary the recording rate based on detection of the behavior of interest by the software. Sub-interval behavior of interest can be masked on occasion (e.g., a 5-minute extreme downpour with high-erosive capability hidden by an innocuous hourly total). Most users prefer measurements that are systematic in time because they are much easier to summarize and manipulate.

For breakpoint data produced by event reporters, there also is a need to send periodically a signal that the station is still functioning, even though there is nothing more to report. "No report" does not necessarily mean "no data," and it is important to distinguish between the actual observation that was recorded and the content of that observation (e.g., an observation of "0.00" is not the same as "no observation").

D.1.6. Mixed Time Scales
There are times when we may wish to combine information from radically different scales. For example, over the past 100 years we may want to know how the frequency of 5-minute precipitation peaks has varied or how the frequency of peak 1-second wind gusts have varied. We may also want to know over this time if nearby vegetation gradually has grown up to increasingly block the wind or to slowly improve precipitation catch. Answers to these questions require knowledge over a wide range of time scales.

D.1.7. Elements
For manual measurements, the typical elements recorded included temperature extremes, precipitation, and snowfall/snow depth. Automated measurements typically include temperature, precipitation, humidity, wind speed and direction, and solar radiation. An exception to this exists in very windy locations where precipitation is difficult to measure accurately. Automated measurements of snow are improving, but manual measurements are still preferable, as long as shielding is present. Automated measurement of frozen precipitation presents numerous challenges that have not been resolved fully, and the best gauges are quite expensive ($3–8K).

Soil temperatures also are included sometimes. Soil moisture is extremely useful, but measurements are not made at many sites. In addition, care must be taken in the installation and maintenance of instruments used in measuring soil moisture. Soil properties vary tremendously in short distances as well, and it is often very difficult ("impossible") to accurately document these variations (without digging up all the soil!). In cooler climates, ultrasonic sensors that detect snow depth are becoming commonplace.

D.1.8. Wind Standards

Wind varies the most in the shortest distance, since it always decreases to zero near the ground and increases rapidly (approximately logarithmically) with height near the ground. Changes in anemometer height obviously will affect distribution of wind speed as will changes in vegetation, obstructions such as buildings, etc. A site that has a 3-m (10-ft) mast clearly will be less windy than a site that has a 6-m (20-ft) or 10-m (33-ft) mast. Historically, many U.S. airports (FAA and NWS) and most current RAWS sites have used a standard 6-m (20-ft) mast for wind measurements. Some NPS RAWS sites utilize shorter masts. Over the last decade, as Automated Surface Observing Systems (ASOSs, mostly NWS) and Automated Weather Observing Systems (AWOSs, mostly FAA) have been deployed at most airports, wind masts have been raised to 8 or 10 m (26 or 33 ft), depending on airplane clearance. The World Meteorological Organization recommends 10 m as the height for wind measurements (WMO 1983; 2005), and more groups are migrating slowly to this standard. The American Association of State Climatologists (AASC 1985) have recommended that wind be measured at 3 m, a standard geared more for agricultural applications than for general purpose uses where higher levels usually are preferred. Different anemometers have different starting thresholds; therefore, areas that frequently experience very light winds may not produce wind measurements thus affecting long-term mean estimates of wind speed. For both sustained winds (averages over a short interval of 2–60 minutes) and especially for gusts, the duration of the sampling interval makes considerable difference. For the same wind history, 1–second gusts are higher than gusts averaging 3 seconds, which in turn are greater than 5-second averages, so that the same sequence would be described with different numbers (all three systems and more are in use). Changes in the averaging procedure, or in height or exposure, can lead to "false" or "fake" climate change with no change in actual climate. Changes in any of these should be noted in the metadata.

D.1.9. Wind Nomenclature

Wind is a vector quantity having a direction and a speed. Directions can be two- or three-dimensional; they will be three-dimensional if the vertical component is important. In all common uses, winds always are denoted by the direction they blow *from* (north wind or southerly breeze). This convention exists because wind often brings weather, and thus our attention is focused upstream. However, this approach contrasts with the way ocean currents are viewed. Ocean currents usually are denoted by the direction they are moving *towards* (eastward current moves from west to east). In specialized applications (such as in atmospheric modeling), wind velocity vectors point in the direction that the wind is blowing. Thus, a southwesterly wind (from the southwest) has both northward and eastward (to the north and to the east) components. Except near mountains, wind cannot blow up or down near the ground, so the vertical component of wind often is approximated as zero, and the horizontal component is emphasized.

D.1.10. Frozen Precipitation

Frozen precipitation is more difficult to measure than liquid precipitation, especially with automated techniques. Sevruk and Harmon (1984), Goodison et al. (1998), and Yang et al. (1998; 2001) provide many of the reasons to explain this. The importance of frozen precipitation varies greatly from one setting to another. This subject was discussed in greater detail in a related inventory and monitoring report for the Alaska park units (Redmond et al. 2005).

In climates that receive frozen precipitation, a decision must be made whether or not to try to record such events accurately. This usually means that the precipitation must be turned into liquid either by falling into an antifreeze fluid solution that is then weighed or by heating the precipitation enough to melt and fall through a measuring mechanism such as a nearly-balanced tipping bucket. Accurate measurements from the first approach require expensive gauges; tipping buckets can achieve this resolution readily but are more apt to lose some or all precipitation. Improvements have been made to the heating mechanism on the NWS tipping-bucket gauge used for the ASOS to correct its numerous deficiencies making it less problematic; however, this gauge is not inexpensive. A heat supply needed to melt frozen precipitation usually requires more energy than renewable energy (solar panels or wind recharging) can provide thus AC power is needed. The availability of AC power is severely limited in many cold or remote U. S. settings. Furthermore, periods of frozen precipitation or rime often provide less-than-optimal recharging conditions with heavy clouds, short days, low-solar-elevation angles and more horizon blocking, and cold temperatures causing additional drain on the battery.

D.1.11. Save or Lose

A second consideration with precipitation is determining if the measurement should be saved (as in weighing systems) or lost (as in tipping-bucket systems). With tipping buckets, after the water has passed through the tipping mechanism, it usually just drops to the ground. Thus, there is no checksum to ensure that the sum of all the tips adds up to what has been saved in a reservoir at some location. By contrast, the weighing gauges continually accumulate until the reservoir is emptied, the reported value is the total reservoir content (for example, the height of the liquid column in a tube), and the incremental precipitation is the difference in depth between two known times. These weighing gauges do not always have the same fine resolution. Some gauges only record to the nearest centimeter, which is usually acceptable for hydrology but not necessarily for other needs. (For reference, a millimeter of precipitation can get a person in street clothes quite wet.) This is how the USDA/NRCS Snowfall Telemetry (SNOTEL) system works in climates that measure up to 3000 cm of snow in a winter. (See http://www.wcc.nrcs.usda.gov/publications for publications or http://www.wcc.nrcs.usda.gov/factpub/aib536.html for a specific description.) No precipitation is lost this way. A thin layer of oil is used to suppress evaporation, and anti-freeze ensures that frozen precipitation melts. When initially recharged, the sum of the oil and starting antifreeze solution is treated as the zero point. The anti-freeze usually is not sufficiently environmentally friendly to discharge to the ground and thus must be hauled into the area and then back out. Other weighing gauges are capable of measuring to the 0.25-mm (0.01-in.) resolution but do not have as much capacity and must be emptied more often. Day/night and storm-related thermal expansion and contraction and sometimes wind shaking can cause fluid pressure from accumulated totals to go up and down in SNOTEL gauges by small increments (commonly 0.3-3 cm, or 0.01–0.10 ft) leading to "negative precipitation" followed by similarly non-real light precipitation when, in fact, no change took place in the amount of accumulated precipitation.

D.1.12. Time

Time should always be in local standard time (LST), and daylight savings time (DST) should never be used under any circumstances with automated equipment and timers. Using DST leads to one duplicate hour, one missing hour, and a season of displaced values, as well as needless confusion and a data-management nightmare. Absolute time, such as Greenwich Mean Time (GMT) or Coordinated Universal Time (UTC), also can be used because these formats are unambiguously translatable. Since measurements only provide information about what already *has* occurred or *is* occurring and not what *will* occur, they should always be assigned to the *ending time* of the associated interval with hour 24 marking the end of the last hour of the day. In this system, midnight always represents the end of the day, not the start. To demonstrate the importance of this differentiation, we have encountered situations where police officers seeking corroborating weather data could not recall whether the time on their crime report from a year ago was the starting midnight or the ending midnight! Station positions should be known to within a few meters, easily accomplished with GPS, so that time zones and solar angles can be determined accurately.

D.1.13. Automated versus Manual

Most of this report has addressed automated measurements. Historically, most measurements are manual and typically collected once a day. In many cases, manual measurements continue because of habit, usefulness, and desire for continuity over time. Manual measurements are extremely useful and when possible should be encouraged. However, automated measurements are becoming more common. For either, it is important to record time in a logically consistent manner.

It should not be automatically assumed that newer data and measurements are "better" than older data or that manual data are "worse" than automated data. Older or simpler manual measurements are often of very high quality even if they sometimes are not in the most convenient digital format.

There is widespread desire to use automated systems to reduce human involvement. This is admirable and understandable, but every automated weather/climate station or network requires significant human attention and maintenance. A telling example concerns the Oklahoma Mesonet (see Brock et al. 1995, and bibliography at http://www.mesonet.ou.edu), a network of about 115 high–quality, automated meteorological stations spread over Oklahoma, where about 80 percent of the annual ($2–3M) budget is nonetheless allocated to humans with only about 20 percent allocated to equipment.

D.1.14. Manual Conventions

Manual measurements typically are made once a day. Elements usually consist of maximum and minimum temperature, temperature at observation time, precipitation, snowfall, snow depth, and sometimes evaporation, wind, or other information. Since it is not actually known when extremes occurred, the only logical approach, and the nationwide convention, is to ascribe the entire measurement to the time-interval date and to enter it on the form in that way. For morning observers (for example, 8 am to 8 am), this means that the maximum temperature written for today often is from yesterday afternoon and sometimes the minimum temperature for the 24-hr period actually occurred yesterday morning. However, this is understood and expected. It is often a surprise to observers to see how many maximum temperatures do not occur in the afternoon and how many minimum temperatures do not occur in the predawn hours. This is especially true in environments that are colder, higher, northerly, cloudy, mountainous, or coastal. As long as this convention is strictly followed every day, it has been shown that truly excellent climate records can result (Redmond 1992). Manual observers should reset equipment only one time per day at the official observing time. Making more than one measurement a day is discouraged strongly; this practice results in a hybrid record that is too difficult to interpret. The only exception is for total daily snowfall. New snowfall can be measured up to four times per day with no observations closer than six hours. It is well known that more frequent measurement of snow increases the annual total because compaction is a continuous process.

Two main purposes for climate observations are to establish the long-term averages for given locations and to track variations in climate. Broadly speaking, these purposes address topics of absolute and relative climate behavior. Once absolute behavior has been "established" (a task that is never finished because long-term averages continue to vary in time)—temporal variability quickly becomes the item of most interest.

D.2. Representativeness

Having discussed important factors to consider when new sites are installed, we now turn our attention to site "representativeness." In popular usage, we often encounter the notion that a site is "representative" of another site if it receives the same annual precipitation or records the same annual temperature or if some other element-specific, long-term average has a similar value. This notion of representativeness has a certain limited validity, but there are other aspects of this idea that need to be considered.

A climate monitoring site also can be said to be representative if climate records from that site show sufficiently strong temporal correlations with a large number of locations over a sufficiently large area. If station A receives 20 cm a year and station B receives 200 cm a year, these climates obviously receive quite differing amounts of precipitation. However, if their monthly, seasonal, or annual correlations are high (for example, 0.80 or higher for a particular time scale), one site can be used as a surrogate for estimating values at the other if measurements for a particular month, season, or year are missing. That is, a wet or dry month at one station is also a wet or dry month (relative to its own mean) at the comparison station. Note that high correlations on one time scale do not imply automatically that high correlations will occur on other time scales.

Likewise, two stations having similar mean climates (for example, similar annual precipitation) might not co-vary in close synchrony (for example, coastal versus interior). This may be considered a matter of climate "affiliation" for a particular location.

Thus, the representativeness of a site can refer either to the basic climatic averages for a given duration (or time window within the annual cycle) or to the extent that the site co-varies in time with respect to all surrounding locations. One site can be representative of another in the first sense but not the second, or vice versa, or neither, or both—all combinations are possible.

If two sites are perfectly correlated then, in a sense, they are "redundant." However, redundancy has value because all sites will experience missing data especially with automated equipment in rugged environments and harsh climates where outages and other problems nearly can be guaranteed. In many cases, those outages are caused by the weather, particularly by unusual weather and the very conditions we most wish to know about. Methods for filling in those values will require proxy information from this or other nearby networks. Thus, redundancy is a virtue rather than a vice.

In general, the cooperative stations managed by the NWS have produced much longer records than automated stations like RAWS or SNOTEL stations. The RAWS stations often have problems with precipitation, especially in winter, or with missing data, so that low correlations may be data problems rather than climatic dissimilarity. The RAWS records also are relatively short, so correlations should be interpreted with care. In performing and interpreting such analyses, however, we must remember that there are physical climate reasons and observational reasons why stations within a short distance (even a few tens or hundreds of meters) may not correlate well.

D.2.1. Temporal Behavior

It is possible that high correlations will occur between station pairs during certain portions of the year (i.e., January) but low correlations may occur during other portions of the year (e.g., September or October). The relative contributions of these seasons to the annual total (for precipitation) or average (for temperature) and the correlations for each month are both factors in the correlation of an aggregated time window of longer duration that encompasses those seasons (e.g., one of the year definitions such as calendar year or water year). A complete and careful evaluation ideally would include such a correlation analysis but requires more resources and data. Note that it also is possible and frequently is observed that temperatures are highly correlated while precipitation is not or vice versa, and these relations can change according to the time of year. If two stations are well correlated for all climate elements for all portions of the year, then they can be considered redundant.

With scarce resources, the initial strategy should be to try to identify locations that do not correlate particularly well, so that each new site measures something new that cannot be guessed easily from the behavior of surrounding sites. (An important caveat here is that lack of such correlation could be a result of physical climate behavior and not a result of faults with the actual measuring process; i.e., by unrepresentative or simply poor-quality data. Unfortunately, we seldom have perfect climate data.) As additional sites are added, we usually wish for some combination of unique and redundant sites to meet what amounts to essentially orthogonal constraints: new information and more reliably-furnished information.

A common consideration is whether to observe on a ridge or in a valley, given the resources to place a single station within a particular area of a few square kilometers. Ridge and valley stations will correlate very well for temperatures when lapse conditions prevail, particularly summer daytime temperatures. In summer at night or winter at daylight, the picture will be more mixed and correlations will be lower. In winter at night when inversions are common and even the rule, correlations may be zero or even negative and perhaps even more divergent as the two sites are on opposite sides of the inversion. If we had the luxury of locating stations everywhere, we would find that ridge tops generally correlate very well with other ridge tops and similarly valleys with other valleys, but ridge tops correlate well with valleys only under certain circumstances. Beyond this, valleys and ridges having similar orientations usually will correlate better with each other than those with perpendicular orientations, depending on their orientation with respect to large-scale wind flow and solar angles.

Unfortunately, we do not have stations everywhere, so we are forced to use the few comparisons that we have and include a large dose of intelligent reasoning, using what we have observed elsewhere. In performing and interpreting such analyses, we must remember that there are physical climatic reasons and observational reasons why stations within a short distance (even a few tens or hundreds of meters) may not correlate well.

Examples of correlation analyses include those for the Channel Islands and for southwest Alaska, which can be found in Redmond and McCurdy (2005) and Redmond et al. (2005). These examples illustrate what can be learned from correlation analyses. Spatial correlations generally vary by time of year. Thus, results should be displayed in the form of annual correlation cycles— for monthly mean temperature and monthly total precipitation and perhaps other climate elements like wind or humidity—between station pairs selected for climatic setting and data availability and quality.

In general, the COOP stations managed by the NWS have produced much longer records than have automated stations like RAWS or SNOTEL stations. The RAWS stations also often have problems with precipitation, especially in winter or with missing data, so that low correlations may be data problems rather than climate dissimilarity. The RAWS records are much shorter, so correlations should be interpreted with care, but these stations are more likely to be in places of interest for remote or under-sampled regions.

D.2.2. Spatial Behavior

A number of techniques exist to interpolate from isolated point values to a spatial domain. For example, a common technique is simple inverse distance weighting. Critical to the success of the simplest of such techniques is that some other property of the spatial domain, one that is influential for the mapped element, does not vary significantly. Topography greatly influences precipitation, temperature, wind, humidity, and most other meteorological elements. Thus, this criterion clearly is not met in any region having extreme topographic diversity. In such circumstances, simple Cartesian distance may have little to do with how rapidly correlation deteriorates from one site to the next, and in fact, the correlations can decrease readily from a mountain to a valley and then increase again on the next mountain. Such structure in the fields of spatial correlation is not seen in the relatively (statistically) well-behaved flat areas like those in the eastern U.S.

To account for dominating effects such as topography and inland–coastal differences that exist in certain regions, some kind of additional knowledge must be brought to bear to produce meaningful, physically plausible, and observationally based interpolations. Historically, this has proven to be an extremely difficult problem, especially to perform objective and repeatable analyses. An analysis performed for southwest Alaska (Redmond et al. 2005) concluded that the PRISM (Parameter Regression on Independent Slopes Model) maps (Daly et al. 1994; 2002; Gibson et al. 2002; Doggett et al. 2004) were probably the best available. An analysis by Simpson et al. (2005) further discussed many issues in the mapping of Alaska's climate and resulted in the same conclusion about PRISM.

D.2.3. Climate-Change Detection

Although general purpose climate stations should be situated to address all aspects of climate variability, it is desirable that they also be in locations that are more sensitive to climate change from natural or anthropogenic influences should it begin to occur. The question here is how well we know such sensitivities. The polar regions are generally regarded as being more sensitive to changes in radiative forcing of climate because of positive feedbacks. The climate-change issue is quite complex because it encompasses more than just greenhouse gasses.

Sites that are in locations or climates particularly vulnerable to climate change should be favored. How this vulnerability is determined is a considerably challenging research issue. Candidate locations or situations are those that lie on the border between two major biomes or just inside the edge of one or the other. In these cases, a slight movement of the boundary in anticipated direction (toward "warmer," for example) would be much easier to detect as the boundary moves past the site and a different set of biota begin to be established. Such a vegetative or ecologic response would be more visible and would take less time to establish as a real change than would a smaller change in the center of the distribution range of a marker or key species.

D.2.4. Element-Specific Differences

The various climate elements (temperature, precipitation, cloudiness, snowfall, humidity, wind speed and direction, solar radiation) do not vary through time in the same sequence or manner nor should they necessarily be expected to vary in this manner. The spatial patterns of variability should not be expected to be the same for all elements. These patterns also should not be expected to be similar for all months or seasons. The suitability of individual sites for measurement also varies from one element to another. A site that has a favorable exposure for temperature or wind may not have a favorable exposure for precipitation or snowfall. A site that experiences proper air movement may be situated in a topographic channel, such as a river valley or a pass, which restricts the range of wind directions and affects the distribution of speed-direction categories.

D.2.5. Logistics and Practical Factors

Even with the most advanced scientific rationale, sites in some remote or climatically challenging settings may not be suitable because of the difficulty in servicing and maintaining equipment. Contributing to these challenges are scheduling difficulties, animal behavior, snow burial, icing, snow behavior, access and logistical problems, and the weather itself. Remote and elevated sites usually require far more attention and expense than a rain-dominated, easily accessible valley location.

For climate purposes, station exposure and the local environment should be maintained in their original state (vegetation especially), so that changes seen are the result of regional climate variations and not of trees growing up, bushes crowding a site, surface albedo changing, fire clearing, etc. Repeat photography has shown many examples of slow environmental change in the vicinity of a station in rather short time frames (5–20 years), and this technique should be employed routinely and frequently at all locations. In the end, logistics, maintenance, and other practical factors almost always determine the success of weather- and climate-monitoring activities.

D.2.6. Personnel Factors

Many past experiences (almost exclusively negative) strongly support the necessity to place primary responsibility for station deployment and maintenance in the hands of seasoned, highly qualified, trained, and meticulously careful personnel, the more experienced the better. Over time, even in "benign" climates but especially where harsher conditions prevail, every conceivable problem will occur and both the usual and unusual should be anticipated: weather, animals, plants, salt, sensor and communication failure, windblown debris, corrosion, power failures, vibrations, avalanches, snow loading and creep, corruption of the data logger program, etc. An ability to anticipate and forestall such problems, a knack for innovation and improvisation, knowledge of electronics, practical and organizational skills, and presence of mind to bring the various small but vital parts, spares, tools, and diagnostic troubleshooting equipment are highly valued qualities. Especially when logistics are so expensive, a premium should be placed on using experienced personnel, since the slightest and seemingly most minor mistake can render a station useless or, even worse, uncertain. Exclusive reliance on individuals without this background can be costly and almost always will result eventually in unnecessary loss of data. Skilled labor and an apprenticeship system to develop new skilled labor will greatly reduce (but not eliminate) the types of problems that can occur in operating a climate network.

D.3. Site Selection

In addition to considerations identified previously in this appendix, various factors need to be considered in selecting sites for new or augmented instrumentation.

D.3.1. Equipment and Exposure Factors

D.3.1.1. Measurement Suite: All sites should measure temperature, humidity, wind, solar radiation, and snow depth. Precipitation measurements are more difficult but probably should be attempted with the understanding that winter measurements may be of limited or no value unless an all-weather gauge has been installed. Even if an all-weather gauge has been installed, it is desirable to have a second gauge present that operates on a different principle–for example, a fluid-based system like those used in the SNOTEL stations in tandem with a higher–resolution, tipping bucket gauge for summertime. Without heating, a tipping bucket gauge usually is of use only when temperatures are above freezing and when temperatures have not been below freezing for some time, so that accumulated ice and snow is not melting and being recorded as present precipitation. Gauge undercatch is a significant issue in snowy climates, so shielding should be considered for all gauges designed to work over the winter months. It is very important to note the presence or absence of shielding, the type of shielding, and the dates of installation or removal of the shielding.

D.3.1.2. Overall Exposure: The ideal, general all-purpose site has gentle slopes, is open to the sun and the wind, has a natural vegetative cover, avoids strong local (less than 200 m) influences, and represents a reasonable compromise among all climate elements. The best temperature sites are not the best precipitation sites, and the same is true for other elements. Steep topography in the immediate vicinity should be avoided unless settings where precipitation is affected by steep topography are being deliberately sought or a mountaintop or ridgeline is the desired location. The potential for disturbance should be considered: fire and flood risk, earth movement, wind-borne debris, volcanic deposits or lahars, vandalism, animal tampering, and general human encroachment are all factors.

D.3.1.3. Elevation: Mountain climates do not vary in time in exactly the same manner as adjoining valley climates. This concept is emphasized when temperature inversions are present to a greater degree and during precipitation when winds rise up the slopes at the same angle. There is considerable concern that mountain climates will be (or already are) changing and perhaps changing differently than lowland climates, which has direct and indirect consequences for plant and animal life in the more extreme zones. Elevations of special significance are those that are near the mean rain/snow line for winter, near the tree line, and near the mean annual freezing level (all of these may not be quite the same). Because the lapse rates in wet climates often are nearly moist-adiabatic during the main precipitation seasons, measurements at one elevation may be extrapolated to nearby elevations. In drier climates and in the winter, temperature and to a lesser extent wind will show various elevation profiles.

D.3.1.4. Transects: The concept of observing transects that span climatic gradients is sound. This is not always straightforward in topographically uneven terrain, but these transects could still be arranged by setting up station(s) along the coast; in or near passes atop the main coastal interior drainage divide; and inland at one, two, or three distances into the interior lowlands. Transects need not—and by dint of topographic constraints probably cannot—be straight lines, but the closer that a line can be approximated the better. The main point is to systematically sample the key points of a behavioral transition without deviating too radically from linearity.

D.3.1.5. Other Topographic Considerations: There are various considerations with respect to local topography. Local topography can influence wind (channeling, upslope/downslope, etc.), precipitation (orographic enhancement, downslope evaporation, catch efficiency, etc.), and temperature (frost pockets, hilltops, aspect, mixing or decoupling from the overlying atmosphere, bowls, radiative effects, etc.), to different degrees at differing scales. In general, for measurements to be areally representative, it is better to avoid these local effects to the extent that they can be identified before station deployment (once deployed, it is desirable not to move a station). The primary purpose of a climate-monitoring network should be to serve as an infrastructure in the form of a set of benchmark stations for comparing other stations. Sometimes, however, it is exactly these local phenomena that we want to capture. Living organisms, especially plants, are affected by their immediate environment, whether it is representative of a larger setting or not. Specific measurements of limited scope and duration made for these purposes then can be tied to the main benchmarks. This experience is useful also in determining the complexity needed in the benchmark monitoring process in order to capture particular phenomena at particular space and time scales.

Sites that drain (cold air) well generally are better than sites that allow cold air to pool. Slightly sloped areas (1 degree is fine) or small benches from tens to hundreds of meters above streams are often favorable locations. Furthermore, these sites often tend to be out of the path of hazards (like floods) and to have rocky outcroppings where controlling vegetation will not be a major concern. Benches or wide spots on the rise between two forks of a river system are often the only flat areas and sometimes jut out to give greater exposure to winds from more directions.

D.3.1.6. Prior History: The starting point in designing a program is to determine what kinds of observations have been collected over time, by whom, in what manner, and if these observation are continuing to the present time. It also may be of value to "re-occupy" the former site of a station that is now inactive to provide some measure of continuity or a reference point from the past. This can be of value even if continuous observations were not made during the entire intervening period.

D.3.2. Element-Specific Factors

D.3.2.1. Temperature: An open exposure with uninhibited air movement is the preferred setting. The most common measurement is made at approximately eye level, 1.5–2.0 m. In snowy locations sensors should be at least one meter higher than the deepest snowpack expected in the next 50 years or perhaps 2–3 times the depth of the average maximum annual depth. Sensors should be shielded above and below from solar radiation (bouncing off snow), from sunrise/sunset horizontal input, and from vertical rock faces. Sensors should be clamped tightly, so that they do not swivel away from level stacks of radiation plates. Nearby vegetation should be kept away from the sensors (several meters). Growing vegetation should be cut to original conditions. Small hollows and swales can cool tremendously at night, and it is best avoid these areas. Side slopes of perhaps a degree or two of angle facilitate air movement and drainage and, in effect, sample a large area during nighttime hours. The very bottom of a valley should be avoided. Temperature can change substantially from moves of only a few meters. Situations have been observed where flat and seemingly uniform conditions (like airport runways) appear to demonstrate different climate behaviors over short distances of a few tens or hundreds of meters (differences of 5–10°C). When snow is on the ground, these microclimatic differences can be stronger, and differences of 2–5°C can occur in the short distance between the thermometer and the snow surface on calm evenings.

D.3.2.2. Precipitation (liquid): Calm locations with vegetative or artificial shielding are preferred. Wind will adversely impact readings; therefore, the less the better. Wind effects on precipitation are far less for rain than for snow. Devices that "save" precipitation present advantages, but most gauges are built to dump precipitation as it falls or to empty periodically. Automated gauges give both the amount and the timing. Simple backups that record only the total precipitation since the last visit have a certain advantage (for example, storage gauges or lengths of PVC pipe perhaps with bladders on the bottom). The following question should be asked: Does the total precipitation from an automated gauge add up to the measured total in a simple bucket (evaporation is prevented with an appropriate substance such as mineral oil)? Drip from overhanging foliage and trees can augment precipitation totals.

D.3.2.3. Precipitation (frozen): Calm locations or shielding are a must. Undercatch for rain is only about 5 percent, but with winds of only 2–4 m/s, gauges may catch only 30–70 percent of the actual snow falling depending on density of the flakes. To catch 100 percent of the snow, the standard configuration for shielding is employed by the CRN: the DFIR (Double-Fence Intercomparison Reference) shield with 2.4-m (8-ft.) vertical, wooden slatted fences in two concentric octagons with diameters of 8 m and 4 m (26 ft and 13 ft, respectively) and an inner Alter shield (flapping vanes). Numerous tests have shown this is the only way to achieve complete catch of snowfall (e.g., Yang et al. 1998, 2001). The DFIR shield is large and bulky; it is recommended that all precipitation gauges have at least Alter shields on them.

Near the coast, much snow is heavy and falls more vertically. In colder locations or storms, light flakes frequently will fly in and then out of the gauge. Clearings in forests are usually excellent sites. Snow blowing from trees that are too close can augment actual precipitation totals. Artificial shielding (vanes, etc.) placed around gauges in snowy locales always should be used if accurate totals are desired. Moving parts tend to freeze up. Capping of gauges during heavy snowfall events is a common occurrence. When the cap becomes pointed, snow falls off to the ground and is not recorded. Caps and plugs often will not fall into the tube until hours, days, or even weeks have passed, typically during an extended period of freezing temperature or above or when sunlight finally occurs. Liquid-based measurements (e.g., SNOTEL "rocket" gauges) do not have the resolution (usually 0.3 cm [0.1 in.] rather than 0.03 cm [0.01 in.]) that tipping bucket and other gauges have but are known to be reasonably accurate in very snowy climates. Light snowfall events might not be recorded until enough of them add up to the next reporting increment. More expensive gauges like Geonors can be considered and could do quite well in snowy settings; however, they need to be emptied every 40 cm (15 in.) or so (capacity of 51 cm [20 in.]) until the new 91-cm (36-in.) capacity gauge is offered for sale. Recently, the NWS has been trying out the new (and very expensive) Ott all-weather gauge. Riming can be an issue in windy foggy environments below freezing. Rime, dew, and other forms of atmospheric condensation are not real precipitation, since they are caused by the gauge.

D.3.2.4. Snow Depth: Windswept areas tend to be blown clear of snow. Conversely, certain types of vegetation can act as a snow fence and cause artificial drifts. However, some amount of vegetation in the vicinity generally can help slow down the wind. The two most common types of snow-depth gauges are the Judd Snow Depth Sensor, produced by Judd Communications, and the snow depth gauge produced by Campbell Scientific, Inc. Opinions vary on which one is better. These gauges use ultrasound and look downward in a cone about 22 degrees in diameter. The ground should be relatively clear of vegetation and maintained in a manner so that the zero point on the calibration scale does not change.

D.3.2.5. Snow Water Equivalent: This is determined by the weight of snow on fluid-filled pads about the size of a desktop set up sometimes in groups of four or in larger hexagons several meters in diameter. These pads require flat ground some distance from nearby sources of windblown snow and shielding that is "just right": not too close to the shielding to act as a kind of snow fence and not too far from the shielding so that blowing and drifting become a factor. Generally, these pads require fluids that possess antifreeze-like properties, as well as handling and replacement protocols.

D.3.2.6. Wind: Open exposures are needed for wind measurements. Small prominences or benches without blockage from certain sectors are preferred. A typical rule for trees is to site stations back 10 tree-heights from all tree obstructions. Sites in long, narrow valleys can obviously only exhibit two main wind directions. Gently rounded eminences are more favored. Any kind of topographic steering should be avoided to the extent possible. Avoiding major mountain chains or single isolated mountains or ridges is usually a favorable approach, if there is a choice. Sustained wind speed and the highest gusts (1-second) should be recorded. Averaging methodologies for both sustained winds and gusts can affect climate trends and should be recorded as metadata with all changes noted. Vegetation growth affects the vertical wind profile, and growth over a few years can lead to changes in mean wind speed even if the "real" wind does not change, so vegetation near the site (perhaps out to 50 m) should be maintained in a quasi-permanent status (same height and spatial distribution). Wind devices can rime up and freeze or spin out of balance. In severely rimed or windy climates, rugged anemometers, such as those made by Taylor, are worth considering. These anemometers are expensive but durable and can withstand substantial abuse. In exposed locations, personnel should plan for winds to be at least 50 m/s and be able to measure these wind speeds. At a minimum, anemometers should be rated to 75 m/s.

D.3.2.7. Humidity: Humidity is a relatively straightforward climate element. Close proximity to lakes or other water features can affect readings. Humidity readings typically are less accurate near 100 percent and at low humidities in cold weather.

D.3.2.8. Solar Radiation: A site with an unobstructed horizon obviously is the most desirable. This generally implies a flat plateau or summit. However, in most locations trees or mountains will obstruct the sun for part of the day.

D.3.2.9. Soil Temperature: It is desirable to measure soil temperature at locations where soil is present. If soil temperature is recorded at only a single depth, the most preferred depth is 10 cm. Other common depths include 25 cm, 50 cm, 2 cm, and 100 cm. Biological activity in the soil will be proportional to temperature with important threshold effects occurring near freezing.

D.3.2.10. Soil Moisture: Soil-moisture gauges are somewhat temperamental and require care to install. The soil should be characterized by a soil expert during installation of the gauge. The readings may require a certain level of experience to interpret correctly. If accurate, readings of soil moisture are especially useful.

D.3.2.11. Distributed Observations: It can be seen readily that compromises must be struck among the considerations described in the preceding paragraphs because some are mutually exclusive.

How large can a "site" be? Generally, the equipment footprint should be kept as small as practical with all components placed next to each other (within less than 10–20 m or so). Readings from one instrument frequently are used to aid in interpreting readings from the remaining instruments.

What is a tolerable degree of separation? Some consideration may be given to locating a precipitation gauge or snow pillow among protective vegetation, while the associated temperature, wind, and humidity readings would be collected more effectively in an open and exposed location within 20–50 m. Ideally, it is advantageous to know the wind measurement precisely at the precipitation gauge, but a compromise involving a short split, and in effect a "distributed observation," could be considered. There are no definitive rules governing this decision, but it is suggested that the site footprint be kept within approximately 50 m. There also are constraints imposed by engineering and electrical factors that affect cable lengths, signal strength, and line noise; therefore, the shorter the cable the better. Practical issues include the need to trench a channel to outlying instruments or to allow lines to lie atop the ground and associated problems with animals, humans, weathering, etc. Separating a precipitation gauge up to 100 m or so from an instrument mast may be an acceptable compromise if other factors are not limiting.

D.3.2.12. Instrument Replacement Schedules: Instruments slowly degrade, and a plan for replacing them with new, refurbished, or recalibrated instruments should be in place. After approximately five years, a systematic change-out procedure should result in replacing most sensors in a network. Certain parts, such as solar radiation sensors, are candidates for annual calibration or change-out. Anemometers tend to degrade as bearings erode or electrical contacts become uneven. Noisy bearings are an indication, and a stethoscope might aid in hearing such noises. Increased internal friction affects the threshold starting speed; once spinning, they tend to function properly. Increases in starting threshold speeds can lead to more zero-wind measurements and thus reduce the reported mean wind speed with no real change in wind properties. A field calibration kit should be developed and taken on all site visits, routine or otherwise. Rain gauges can be tested with drip testers during field visits. Protective conduit and tight water seals can prevent abrasion and moisture problems with the equipment, although seals can keep moisture in as well as out. Bulletproof casings sometimes are employed in remote settings. A supply of spare parts, at least one of each and more for less-expensive or more-delicate sensors, should be maintained to allow replacement of worn or nonfunctional instruments during field visits. In addition, this approach allows instruments to be calibrated in the relative convenience of the operational home—the larger the network, the greater the need for a parts depot.

D.3.3. Long-Term Comparability and Consistency

D.3.3.1. Consistency: The emphasis here is to hold biases constant. Every site has biases, problems, and idiosyncrasies of one sort or another. The best rule to follow is simply to try to keep biases constant through time. Since the goal is to track climate through time, keeping sensors, methodologies, and exposure constant will ensure that only true climate change is being measured. This means leaving the site in its original state or performing maintenance to keep it that way. Once a site is installed, the goal should be to never move the site even by a few meters or to allow significant changes to occur within 100 m for the next several decades.

Sites in or near rock outcroppings likely will experience less vegetative disturbance or growth through the years and will not usually retain moisture, a factor that could speed corrosion. Sites that will remain locally similar for some time are usually preferable. However, in some cases the intent of a station might be to record the local climate effects of changes within a small-scale system (for example, glacier, recently burned area, or scene of some other disturbance) that is subject to a regional climate influence. In this example, the local changes might be much larger than the regional changes.

D.3.3.2. Metadata: Since the climate of every site is affected by features in the immediate vicinity, it is vital to record this information over time and to update the record repeatedly at each service visit. Distances, angles, heights of vegetation, fine-scale topography, condition of instruments, shielding discoloration, and other factors from within a meter to several kilometers should be noted. Systematic photography should be undertaken and updated at least once every one–two years.

Photographic documentation should be taken at each site in a standard manner and repeated every two–three years. Guidelines for methodology were developed by Redmond (2004) as a result of experience with the NOAA CRN and can be found on the WRCC NPS Web pages at http://www.wrcc.dri.edu/nps and at ftp://ftp.wrcc.dri.edu/nps/photodocumentation.pdf.

The main purpose for climate stations is to *track climatic conditions through time*. Anything that affects the interpretation of records through time must to be noted and recorded for posterity. The important factors should be clear to a person who has never visited the site, no matter how long ago the site was installed.

In regions with significant, climatic transition zones, transects are an efficient way to span several climates and make use of available resources. Discussions on this topic at greater detail can be found in Redmond and Simeral (2004) and in Redmond et al. (2005).

D.4. Literature Cited

American Association of State Climatologists. 1985. Heights and exposure standards for sensors on automated weather stations. The State Climatologist **9**.

Brock, F. V., K. C. Crawford, R. L. Elliott, G. W. Cuperus, S. J. Stadler, H. L. Johnson and M. D. Eilts. 1995. The Oklahoma Mesonet: A technical overview. Journal of Atmospheric and Oceanic Technology **12**:5-19.

Daly, C., R. P. Neilson, and D. L. Phillips. 1994. A statistical-topographic model for mapping climatological precipitation over mountainous terrain. Journal of Applied Meteorology **33**:140-158.

Daly, C., W. P. Gibson, G. H. Taylor, G. L. Johnson, and P. Pasteris. 2002. A knowledge-based approach to the statistical mapping of climate. Climate Research **22**:99-113.

Doggett, M., C. Daly, J. Smith, W. Gibson, G. Taylor, G. Johnson, and P. Pasteris. 2004. High-resolution 1971-2000 mean monthly temperature maps for the western United States. Fourteenth AMS Conf. on Applied Climatology, 84th AMS Annual Meeting. Seattle, WA, American Meteorological Society, Boston, MA, January 2004, Paper 4.3, CD-ROM.

Geiger, R., R. H. Aron, and P. E. Todhunter. 2003. The Climate Near the Ground. 6th edition. Rowman & Littlefield Publishers, Inc., New York.

Gibson, W. P., C. Daly, T. Kittel, D. Nychka, C. Johns, N. Rosenbloom, A. McNab, and G. Taylor. 2002. Development of a 103-year high-resolution climate data set for the conterminous United States. Thirteenth AMS Conf. on Applied Climatology. Portland, OR, American Meteorological Society, Boston, MA, May 2002:181-183.

Goodison, B. E., P. Y. T. Louie, and D. Yang. 1998. WMO solid precipitation measurement intercomparison final report. WMO TD 982, World Meteorological Organization, Geneva, Switzerland.

National Research Council. 1998. Future of the National Weather Service Cooperative Weather Network. National Academies Press, Washington, D.C.

National Research Council. 2001. A Climate Services Vision: First Steps Toward the Future. National Academies Press, Washington, D.C.

Redmond, K. T. 1992. Effects of observation time on interpretation of climatic time series - A need for consistency. Eighth Annual Pacific Climate (PACLIM) Workshop. Pacific Grove, CA, March 1991:141-150.

Redmond, K. T. 2004. Photographic documentation of long-term climate stations. Available from ftp://ftp.wrcc.dri.edu/nps/photodocumentation.pdf. (accessed 15 August 2004)

Redmond, K. T. and D. B. Simeral. 2004. Climate monitoring comments: Central Alaska Network Inventory and Monitoring Program. Available from ftp://ftp.wrcc.dri.edu/nps/alaska/cakn/npscakncomments040406.pdf. (accessed 6 April 2004)

Redmond, K. T., D. B. Simeral, and G. D. McCurdy. 2005. Climate monitoring for southwest Alaska national parks: network design and site selection. Report 05-01. Western Regional Climate Center, Reno, Nevada.

Redmond, K. T., and G. D. McCurdy. 2005. Channel Islands National Park: Design considerations for weather and climate monitoring. Report 05-02. Western Regional Climate Center, Reno, Nevada.

Sevruk, B., and W. R. Hamon. 1984. International comparison of national precipitation gauges with a reference pit gauge. Instruments and Observing Methods, Report No 17, WMO/TD – 38, World Meteorological Organization, Geneva, Switzerland.

Simpson, J. J., Hufford, G. L., C. Daly, J. S. Berg, and M. D. Fleming. 2005. Comparing maps of mean monthly surface temperature and precipitation for Alaska and adjacent areas of Canada produced by two different methods. Arctic **58**:137-161.

Whiteman, C. D. 2000. Mountain Meteorology: Fundamentals and Applications. Oxford University Press, Oxford, UK.

Wilson, E. O. 1998. Consilience: The Unity of Knowledge. Knopf, New York.

World Meteorological Organization. 1983. Guide to meteorological instruments and methods of observation, No. 8, 5th edition, World Meteorological Organization, Geneva Switzerland.

World Meteorological Organization. 2005. Organization and planning of intercomparisons of rainfall intensity gauges. World Meteorological Organization, Geneva Switzerland.

Yang, D., B. E. Goodison, J. R. Metcalfe, V. S. Golubev, R. Bates, T. Pangburn, and C. Hanson. 1998. Accuracy of NWS 8" standard nonrecording precipitation gauge: results and application of WMO intercomparison. Journal of Atmospheric and Oceanic Technology **15**:54-68.

Yang, D., B. E. Goodison, J. R. Metcalfe, P. Louie, E. Elomaa, C. Hanson, V. Bolubev, T. Gunther, J. Milkovic, and M. Lapin. 2001. Compatibility evaluation of national precipitation gauge measurements. Journal of Geophysical Research **106**:1481-1491.

Appendix E. Master metadata field list

Field Name	Field Type	Field Description
begin_date	date	Effective beginning date for a record.
begin_date_flag	char(2)	Flag describing the known accuracy of the begin date for a station.
best_elevation	float(4)	Best known elevation for a station (in feet).
clim_div_code	char(2)	Foreign key defining climate division code (primary in table: clim_div).
clim_div_key	int2	Foreign key defining climate division for a station (primary in table: clim_div.
clim_div_name	varchar(30)	English name for a climate division.
controller_info	varchar(50)	Person or organization who maintains the identifier system for a given weather or climate network.
country_key	int2	Foreign key defining country where a station resides (primary in table: none).
county_key	int2	Foreign key defining county where a station resides (primary in table: county).
county_name	varchar(31)	English name for a county.
description	text	Any description pertaining to the particular table.
end_date	date	Last effective date for a record.
end_date_flag	char(2)	Flag describing the known accuracy of station end date.
fips_country_code	char(2)	FIPS (federal information processing standards) country code.
fips_state_abbr	char(2)	FIPS state abbreviation for a station.
fips_state_code	char(2)	FIPS state code for a station.
history_flag	char(2)	Describes temporal significance of an individual record among others from the same station.
id_type_key	int2	Foreign key defining the id_type for a station (usually defined in code).
last_updated	date	Date of last update for a record.
latitude	float(8)	Latitude value.
longitude	float(8)	Longitude value.
name_type_key	int2	"3": COOP station name, "2": best station name.
name	varchar(30)	Station name as known at date of last update entry.
ncdc_state_code	char(2)	NCDC, two-character code identifying U.S. state.
network_code	char(8)	Eight-character abbreviation code identifying a network.
network_key	int2	Foreign key defining the network for a station (primary in table: network).
network_station_id	int4	Identifier for a station in the associated network, which is defined by id_type_key.
remark	varchar(254)	Additional information for a record.
src_quality_code	char(2)	Code describing the data quality for the data source.
state_key	int2	Foreign key defining the U.S. state where a station resides (primary in table: state).
state_name	varchar(30)	English name for a state.
station_alt_name	varchar(30)	Other English names for a station.
station_best_name	varchar(30)	Best, most well-known English name for a station.
time_zone	float4	Time zone where a station resides.
ucan_station_id	int4	Unique station identifier for every station in ACIS.
unit_key	int2	Integer value representing a unit of measure.

Field Name	Field Type	Field Description
updated_by	char(8)	Person who last updated a record.
var_major_id	int2	Defines major climate variable.
var_minor_id	int2	Defines data source within a var_major_id.
zipcode	char(5)	Zipcode where a latitude/longitude point resides.
nps_netcode	char(4)	Network four-character identifier.
nps_netname	varchar(128)	Displayed English name for a network.
parkcode	char(4)	Park four-character identifier.
parkname	varchar(128)	Displayed English name for a park/
im_network	char(4)	NPS I&M network where park belongs (a net code)/
station_id	varchar(16)	Station identifier.
station_id_type	varchar(16)	Type of station identifier.
network.subnetwork.id	varchar(16)	Identifier of a sub-network in associated network.
subnetwork_key	int2	Foreign key defining sub-network for a station.
subnetwork_name	varchar(30)	English name for a sub-network.
slope	integer	Terrain slope at the location.
aspect	integer	Terrain aspect at the station.
gps	char(1)	Indicator of latitude/longitude recorded via GPS (global positioning system).
site_description	text(0)	Physical description of site.
route_directions	text(0)	Driving route or site access directions.
station_photo_id	integer	Unique identifier associating a group of photos to a station. Group of photos all taken on same date.
photo_id	char(30)	Unique identifier for a photo.
photo_date	datetime	Date photograph taken.
photographer	varchar(64)	Name of photographer.
maintenance_date	datetime	Date of station maintenance visit.
contact_key	Integer	Unique identifier associating contact information to a station.
full_name	varchar(64)	Full name of contact person.
organization	varchar(64)	Organization of contact person.
contact_type	varchar(32)	Type of contact person (operator, administrator, etc.)
position_title	varchar(32)	Title of contact person.
address	varchar(32)	Address for contact person.
city	varchar(32)	City for contact person.
state	varchar(2)	State for contact person.
zip_code	char(10)	Zipcode for contact person.
country	varchar(32)	Country for contact person.
email	varchar(64)	E-mail for contact person.
work_phone	varchar(16)	Work phone for contact person.
contact_notes	text(254)	Other details regarding contact person.
equipment_type	char(30)	Sensor measurement type; i.e., wind speed, air temperature, etc.
eq_manufacturer	char(30)	Manufacturer of equipment.
eq_model	char(20)	Model number of equipment.
serial_num	char(20)	Serial number of equipment.
eq_description	varchar(254)	Description of equipment.
install_date	datetime	Installation date of equipment.
remove_date	datetime	Removal date of equipment.
ref_height	integer	Sensor displacement height from surface.
sampling_interval	varchar(10)	Frequency of sensor measurement.

Appendix F. Electronic supplements

F.1. ACIS metadata file for weather and climate stations associated with the GULN:
http://www.wrcc.dri.edu/nps/pub/GULN/metadata/GULN_from_ACIS.tar.gz.

F.2. GULN metadata files for weather and climate stations associated with the GULN:
http://www.wrcc.dri.edu/nps/pub/GULN/metadata/GULN_NPS.tar.gz.

Appendix G. Descriptions of weather/climate monitoring networks

G.1. Clean Air Status and Trends Network (CASTNet)

- Purpose of network: provide information for evaluating the effectiveness of national emission-control strategies.
- Primary management agency: EPA.
- Data website: http://epa.gov/castnet/.
- Measured weather/climate elements:
  o Air temperature.
  o Precipitation.
  o Relative humidity.
  o Wind speed.
  o Wind direction.
  o Wind gust.
  o Gust direction.
  o Solar radiation.
  o Soil moisture and temperature.
- Sampling frequency: hourly.
- Reporting frequency: hourly.
- Estimated station cost: $13000.
- Network strengths:
  o High-quality data.
  o Sites are well maintained.
- Network weaknesses:
  o Density of station coverage is low.
  o Shorter periods of record for western U.S.

CASTNet primarily is an air-quality-monitoring network managed by the EPA. The elements shown here are intended to support interpretation of measured air-quality parameters such as ozone, nitrates, sulfides, etc., which also are measured at CASTNet sites.

G.2. NWS Cooperative Observer Program (COOP)

- Purpose of network:
  o Provide observational, meteorological data required to define U.S. climate and help measure long-term climate changes.
  o Provide observational, meteorological data in near real-time to support forecasting and warning mechanisms and other public service programs of the NWS.
- Primary management agency: NOAA (NWS).
- Data website: data are available from the NCDC (http://www.ncdc.noaa.gov), RCCs (e.g., WRCC, http://www.wrcc.dri.edu), and state climate offices.
- Measured weather/climate elements:
  o Maximum, minimum, and observation-time temperature.
  o Precipitation, snowfall, snow depth.

o Pan evaporation (some stations).
- Sampling frequency: daily.
- Reporting frequency: daily or monthly (station-dependent).
- Estimated station cost: $2000 with maintenance costs of $500–900/year.
- Network strengths:
  o Decade–century records at most sites.
  o Widespread national coverage (thousands of stations).
  o Excellent data quality when well maintained.
  o Relatively inexpensive; highly cost effective.
  o Manual measurements; not automated.
- Network weaknesses:
  o Uneven exposures; many are not well-maintained.
  o Dependence on schedules for volunteer observers.
  o Slow entry of data from many stations into national archives.
  o Data subject to observational methodology; not always documented.
  o Manual measurements; not automated and not hourly.

The COOP network has long served as the main climate observation network in the U.S. Readings are usually made by volunteers using equipment supplied, installed, and maintained by the federal government. The observer in effect acts as a host for the data-gathering activities and supplies the labor; this is truly a "cooperative" effort. The SAO sites often are considered to be part of the cooperative network as well if they collect the previously mentioned types of weather/climate observations. Typical observation days are morning to morning, evening to evening, or midnight to midnight. By convention, observations are ascribed to the date the instrument was reset at the end of the observational period. For this reason, midnight observations represent the end of a day. The Historical Climate Network is a subset of the cooperative network but contains longer and more complete records.

G.3. NOAA Climate Reference Network (CRN)

- Purpose of network: provide long-term homogeneous measurements of temperature and precipitation that can be coupled with long-term historic observations to monitor present and future climate change.
- Primary management agency: NOAA.
- Data website: http://www.ncdc.noaa.gov/crn/.
- Measured weather/climate elements:
  o Air temperature (triply redundant, aspirated).
  o Precipitation (three-wire Geonor gauge).
  o Wind speed.
  o Solar radiation.
  o Ground surface temperature.
- Sampling frequency: precipitation can be sampled either 5 or 15 minutes. Temperature sampled every 5 minutes. All other elements sampled every 15 minutes.
- Reporting frequency: hourly or every three hours.
- Estimated station cost: $30000 with maintenance costs around $2000/year.
- Network strengths:

o Station siting is excellent (appropriate for long-term climate monitoring).
o Data quality is excellent.
o Site maintenance is excellent.
- Network weaknesses:
  o CRN network is still developing.
  o Period of record is short compared to other automated networks.
  o Station coverage is limited.
  o Not intended for snowy climates.

Data from the CRN are used in operational climate-monitoring activities and are used to place current climate patterns into a historic perspective. The CRN is intended as a reference network for the U.S. that meets the requirements of the Global Climate Observing System. Up to 115 CRN sites are planned for installation, but the actual number of installed sites will depend on available funding.

G.4. Citizen Weather Observer Program (CWOP)

- Purpose of network: collect observations from private citizens and make these data available for homeland security and other weather applications, providing constant feedback to the observers to maintain high data quality.
- Primary management agency: NOAA MADIS program.
- Data Website: http://www.wxqa.com.
- Measured weather/climate elements:
  o Air temperature.
  o Dewpoint temperature.
  o Precipitation.
  o Wind speed and direction.
  o Barometric pressure.
- Sampling frequency: 15 minutes or less.
- Reporting frequency: 15 minutes.
- Estimated station cost: unknown.
- Network strengths:
  o Active partnership between public agencies and private citizens.
  o Large number of participant sites.
  o Regular communications between data providers and users, encouraging higher data quality.
- Network weaknesses:
  o Variable instrumentation platforms.
  o Metadata are sometimes limited.

The CWOP network is a public-private partnership with U.S. citizens and various agencies including NOAA, NASA (National Aeronautics and Space Administration), and various universities. There are over 4500 registered sites worldwide, with close to 3000 of these sites located in North America.

G.5. NPS Gaseous Pollutant Monitoring Program (GPMP)

- Purpose of network: measurement of ozone and related meteorological elements.
- Primary management agency: NPS.
- Data website: http://www2.nature.nps.gov/air/monitoring.
- Measured weather/climate elements:
  - Air temperature.
  - Relative humidity.
  - Precipitation.
  - Wind speed and direction.
  - Solar radiation.
  - Surface wetness.
- Sampling frequency: continuous.
- Reporting frequency: hourly.
- Estimated station cost: unknown.
- Network strengths:
  - Stations are located within NPS park units.
  - Data quality is excellent, with high data standards.
  - Provides unique measurements that are not available elsewhere.
  - Records are up to 2 decades in length.
  - Site maintenance is excellent.
  - Thermometers are aspirated.
- Network weaknesses:
  - Not easy to download the entire data set or to ingest live data.
  - Period of record is short compared to other automated networks. Earliest sites date from 2004.
  - Station spacing and coverage: station installation is episodic, driven by opportunistic situations.

The NPS web site indicates that there are 33 sites with continuous ozone analysis run by NPS, with records from a few to about 16-17 years. Of these stations, 12 are labeled as GPMP sites and the rest are labeled as CASTNet sites. All of these have standard meteorological measurements, including a 10-m mast. Another nine GPMP sites are located within NPS units but run by cooperating agencies. A number of other sites (1-2 dozen) ran for differing periods in the past, generally less than 5-10 years.

G.6. NOAA Ground-Based GPS Meteorology (GPS-MET) Network

- Purpose of network:
  - Measure atmospheric water vapor using ground-based GPS receivers.
  - Facilitate use of these data operational and in other research and applications.
  - Provides data for weather forecasting, atmospheric modeling and prediction, climate monitoring, calibrating and validation other observing systems including radiosondes and satellites, and research.
- Primary management agency: NOAA Earth System Research Laboratory.
- Data website: http://gpsmet.noaa.gov/jsp/index.jsp.

- Measurements:
  - Dual frequency carrier phase measurements every 30 seconds.
- Ancillary weather/climate observations:
  - Air temperature.
  - Relative humidity.
  - Pressure.
- Reporting frequency: currently 30 min.
- Estimated station cost: $0-$10000, depending on approach. Data from dual frequency GPS receivers installed for conventional applications (e.g. high accuracy surveying) can be used without modification.
- Network strengths:
  - Frequent, high-quality measurements.
  - High reliability.
  - All-weather operability.
  - Many uses.
  - Highly leveraged.
  - Requires no calibration.
  - Measurement accuracy improves with time.
- Network weakness:
  - Point measurement.
  - Provides no direct information about the vertical distribution of water vapor.

The GPS-MET network is the first network of its kind dedicated to GPS meteorology (see Duan et al. 1996). The GPS-MET network was developed in response to the need for improved moisture observations to support weather forecasting, climate monitoring, and other research activities. GPS-MET is a collaboration between NOAA and several other governmental and university organizations and institutions.

GPS meteorology utilizes the radio signals broadcast by the satellite Global Positioning System for atmospheric remote sensing. GPS meteorology applications have evolved along two paths: ground-based (Bevis et al. 1992) and space-based (Yuan et al. 1993). Both applications make the same fundamental measurement (the apparent delay in the arrival of radio signals caused by changes in the radio-refractivity of the atmosphere along the paths of the radio signals) but they do so from different perspectives.

In ground-based GPS meteorology, a GPS receiver and antenna are placed at a fixed location on the ground and the signals from all GPS satellites in view are continuously recorded. From this information, the exact position of the GPS antenna can be determined over time with high (millimeter-level) accuracy. Subsequent measurements of the antenna position are compared with the known position, and the differences can be attributed to changes in the temperature, pressure and water vapor in the atmosphere above the antenna. By making continuous measurements of temperature and pressure at the site, the total amount of water vapor in the atmosphere at this location can be estimated with high accuracy under all weather conditions. For more information on ground based GPS meteorology the reader is referred to http://gpsmet.noaa.gov.

In space-based GPS meteorology, GPS receivers and antennas are placed on satellites in Low Earth Orbit (LEO), and the signals transmitted by a GPS satellite are continuously recorded as a GPS satellite "rises" or "sets" behind the limb of the Earth. This process is called an occultation or a limb sounding. The GPS radio signals bend more as they encounter a thicker atmosphere and the bending (which causes an apparent increase in the length of the path of the radio signal) can be attributed to changes in temperature, pressure and water vapor along the path of the radio signal through the atmosphere that is nominally about 300 km long. The location of an occultation depends on the relative geometries of the GPS satellites in Mid Earth Orbit and the satellites in LEO. As a consequence, information about the vertical temperature, pressure and moisture structure of the Earth's atmosphere as a whole can be estimated with high accuracy, but not at any one particular place over time. The main difference between ground and space-based GPS meteorology is one of geometry. A space-based measurement can be thought of as a ground-based measurement turned on its side. For more information on space based GPS meteorology, the reader is referred to http://www.cosmic.ucar.edu/gpsmet/.

G.7. National Atmospheric Deposition Program (NADP)

- Purpose of network: measurement of precipitation chemistry and atmospheric deposition.
- Primary management agencies: USDA, but multiple collaborators.
- Data website: http://nadp.sws.uiuc.edu.
- Measured weather/climate elements:
  o Precipitation.
- Sampling frequency: daily.
- Reporting frequency: daily.
- Estimated station cost: unknown.
- Network strengths:
  o Data quality is excellent, with high data standards.
  o Site maintenance is excellent.
- Network weaknesses:
  o A very limited number of climate parameters are measured.

Stations within the NADP network monitor primarily wet deposition through precipitation chemistry at selected sites around the U.S. and its territories. The network is a collaborative effort among several agencies including USGS and USDA. Precipitation is the primary climate parameter measured at NADP sites.

G.8. Portable Ozone Monitoring System (POMS)

- Purpose of network: provide seasonal, short-term (1-5 years) monitoring of near-surface atmospheric ozone levels in remote locations.
- Primary management agency: NPS.
- Data website: http://www2.nature.nps.gov/air/studies/portO3.htm.
- Measured weather/climate elements:
  o Air temperature.
  o Precipitation.
  o Relative humidity.
  o Wind speed and direction.

- o Solar radiation.
- Sampling frequency: hourly.
- Reporting frequency: hourly.
- Estimated station cost: $20000 with operation and maintenance costs of up to $10000/year.
- Network strengths:
  - o High-quality data.
  - o Site maintenance is excellent.
- Network weaknesses:
  - o No long-term sites, so not as useful for climate monitoring.
  - o Sites are somewhat expensive to operate.

The POMS network is operated by the NPS Air Resources Division. Sites are intended primarily for summer, short-term (1-5 years) monitoring of near-surface atmospheric ozone levels in remote locations. Measured meteorological elements include temperature, precipitation, wind, relative humidity, and solar radiation.

G.9. Remote Automated Weather Station Network (RAWS)

- Purpose of network: provide near-real-time (hourly or near hourly) measurements of meteorological variables for use in fire weather forecasts and climatology. Data from RAWS also are used for natural resource management, flood forecasting, natural hazard management, and air-quality monitoring.
- Primary management agency: WRCC, National Interagency Fire Center.
- Data website: http://www.raws.dri.edu/index.html.
- Measured weather/climate elements:
  - o Air temperature.
  - o Precipitation.
  - o Relative humidity.
  - o Wind speed.
  - o Wind direction.
  - o Wind gust.
  - o Gust direction.
  - o Solar radiation.
  - o Soil moisture and temperature.
- Sampling frequency: 1 or 10 minutes, element-dependent.
- Reporting frequency: generally hourly. Some stations report every 15 or 30 minutes.
- Estimated station cost: $12000 with satellite telemetry ($8000 without satellite telemetry); maintenance costs are around $2000/year.
- Network strengths:
  - o Metadata records are usually complete.
  - o Sites are located in remote areas.
  - o Sites are generally well-maintained.
  - o Entire period of record available on-line.
- Network weaknesses:
  - o RAWS network is focused largely on fire management needs (formerly focused only on fire needs).

o Frozen precipitation is not measured reliably.

o Station operation is not always continuous.

o Data transmission is completed via one-way telemetry. Data are therefore recoverable either in real-time or not at all.

The RAWS network is used by many land-management agencies, such as the BLM, NPS, Fish and Wildlife Service, Bureau of Indian Affairs, Forest Service, and other agencies. The RAWS network was one of the first automated weather station networks to be installed in the U.S. Most gauges do not have heaters, so hydrologic measurements are of little value when temperatures dip below freezing or reach freezing after frozen precipitation events. There are approximately 1100 real-time sites in this network and about 1800 historic sites (some are decommissioned or moved). The sites can transmit data all winter but may be in deep snow in some locations. The WRCC is the archive for this network and receives station data and metadata through a special connection to the National Interagency Fire Center in Boise, Idaho.

G.10. NWS/FAA Surface Airways Observation Network (SAO)

- Purpose of network: provide near-real-time measurements of meteorological variables and are used both for airport operations and weather forecasting.
- Primary management agency: NOAA, FAA.
- Data website: data are available from state climate offices, RCCs (e.g., WRCC, http://www.wrcc.dri.edu), and NCDC (http://www.ncdc.noaa.gov).
- Measured weather/climate elements:
  o Air temperature.
  o Dewpoint and/or relative humidity.
  o Wind speed.
  o Wind direction.
  o Wind gust.
  o Gust direction.
  o Barometric pressure.
  o Precipitation (not at many FAA sites).
  o Sky cover.
  o Ceiling (cloud height).
  o Visibility.
- Sampling frequency: element-dependent.
- Reporting frequency: element-dependent.
- Estimated station cost: $100000–$200000, with maintenance costs approximately $10000/year.
- Network strengths:
  o Records generally extend over several decades.
  o Consistent maintenance and station operations.
  o Data record is reasonably complete and usually high quality.
  o Hourly or sub-hourly data.
- Network weaknesses:
  o Nearly all sites are located at airports.
  o Data quality can be related to size of airport—smaller airports tend to have poorer

datasets.
o Influences from urbanization and other land-use changes.

These stations are managed by NOAA, U. S. Navy, U. S. Air Force, and FAA. These stations are located generally at major airports and military bases. The FAA stations often do not record precipitation, or they may provide precipitation records of reduced quality. Automated stations are typically ASOSs for the NWS or AWOSs for the FAA. Some sites only report episodically with observers paid per observation.

G.11. USDA/NRCS Soil Climate Analysis Network (SCAN)

- Purpose of network: comprehensive soil-climate network used in natural resource assessments and other conservation activities in the U.S.
- Primary management agency: USDA/NRCS.
- Data website: http://www.wcc.nrcs.usda.gov/scan/.
- Measured weather/climate elements:
  o Air temperature.
  o Precipitation.
  o Relative humidity.
  o Wind speed.
  o Wind direction.
  o Barometric pressure.
  o Solar radiation.
  o Snow water content.
  o Snow depth.
  o Soil moisture and temperature (enhanced sites only).
- Sampling frequency: 1-minute temperature; 1-hour precipitation, snow water content, and snow depth. Less than one minute for relative humidity, wind speed and direction, solar radiation, and soil moisture and temperature (all at enhanced site configurations only).
- Reporting frequency: reporting intervals are user-selectable. Commonly used intervals are every one, two, three, or six hours.
- Estimated station cost: $25000, with maintenance costs approximately $1000/year.
- Network strengths:
  o Sites are well-maintained.
  o Data are of high quality and are largely complete.
  o Very reliable automated system.
- Network weaknesses:
  o Short data records.
  o Network is still in development.

The SCAN network is intended to be a comprehensive nationwide soil moisture and climate information system to be used in supporting natural resource assessments and other conservation activities. These stations are usually located in the agricultural areas of the U.S. All SCAN sites are automated. The parameters measured at these sites include air temperature, precipitation, humidity, wind, pressure, solar radiation, snow depth, and snow water content.

G.12. Weather For You Network (WX4U)

- Purpose of network: allow volunteer weather enthusiasts around the U.S. to observe and share weather data.
- Data website: http://www.met.utah.edu/jhorel/html/mesonet.
- Measured weather/climate elements:
  - Air temperature.
  - Relative humidity and dewpoint temperature.
  - Precipitation.
  - Wind speed and direction.
  - Wind gust and direction.
  - Pressure.
- Sampling frequency: 10 minutes.
- Reporting frequency: 10 minutes.
- Estimated station cost: unknown.
- Network strengths:
  - Stations are located throughout the U.S.
  - Stations provide near-real-time observations.
- Network weaknesses:
  - Instrumentation platforms can be variable.
  - Data are sometimes of questionable quality.

The WX4U network is a nationwide collection of weather stations run by local observers. Meteorological elements that are measured usually include temperature, precipitation, wind, and humidity.

NPS/GULN/NRTR—2007/011, April 2007

www.ingramcontent.com/pod-product-compliance
Lightning Source LLC
Chambersburg PA
CBHW081112290526
45795CB00006B/2091